VILLAGE VOICES

telling of Levisham life
a century ago

VILLAGE VOICES

telling of Levisham life
a century ago

based on

The Rector's Son or Memoirs of John Skelton. 1833
Recollections of the Walker sisters in Levisham 1857-1868
Diary of John Brough 1913

by
Betty Halse

I.S.B.N. No. 0 9530717 0 7

Published by
Moors Publications
Levisham

Designed and printed by
Maxiprint
York, England

INTRODUCTION

What was it like to live in Levisham a century ago?

This tiny village on the edge of the North York Moors still has the same layout as on the 1848 Tithe Map, but is anything else the same? What can be known about the life that went on in the 30 or so households living within the parish boundaries, from the mill down by the stream in the bottom of the steep valley to the east, to the farms and cottages by Newton beck in the valley to the west, with the houses and cottages lining the village street between?

There are three voices we can listen to - voices of people who lived in Levisham and recorded their own accounts of their experiences of life there during the nineteenth, and early years of the twentieth, centuries.

First, we hear from the daughters of James Walker who bought the Manor of Levisham in 1856 and lived with his family in Levisham Hall for around ten years while trying to develop iron mining in Newtondale. His venture failed; he left Levisham and returned to Leeds. Much later, his daughters published two little books about their early lives including the Levisham years. In extracts from these we can hear how the village and its life looked to the children of the Hall.

Go back a generation. Walker had bought Levisham Hall from Robert Skelton, Rector and Lord of the Manor, whose younger brother John was in 1821 caught up in the Methodist revival that was sweeping through the area. After his conversion, he kept a journal which, following his early death, was used as the source for a little tract about him entitled " The Rector's Son; or Memoirs of Mr.John Skelton, late of Levisham". It is of interest for what it tells about the Skelton family who were prominent in the village from the time Robert and John's father came as Rector in 1786, and for the insight it gives into the powerful effect of evangelical religion during the 1820's.

Finally we move on to the year 1913, and the diary in which John Brough, a farm worker, kept a daily record of his tough life on William Keath's farm. Levisham is above all a farming community, so it is appropriate that this should form the most substantial part of the book. His diary reveals the day-to-day reality behind statistics or general accounts of farming before the first world war.

From these three different sources come first-hand impressions of different aspects of the life of the village and the people who lived in it.

Contents

List of Illustrations

Acknowledgements

I wish to thank all those whose interest in Levisham has encouraged and helped me.

John Brough provided the transcript of his father's diary, together with photographs and further information on his father's life.

Mrs H.M.Allanson, Mr & Mrs K. Cooper, Mrs. J.A. Pickup, Mrs N. Sykes and Mrs D. Turnbull kindly lent photographs.

The Sydney Smith photographs (pp.5,10 & 14) are published with kind permission of the Beck Isle Museum, Pickering; the Raymond Hayes photograph (p.V) with permission of the Museum of Rural Life, Hutton le Hole.

SECTION 1

LEVISHAM THROUGH THE EYES
OF THE WALKER SISTERS.

THE WALKER FAMILY AND WALKER'S PIT

On January 19th 1856, a notice appeared in the Yorkshire Gazette offering for sale by auction Levisham Manor - the Hall, land, cottages, farms. It seems that Robert Skelton, Rector and Lord of the Manor, was in financial difficulties and needed to realise his assets by selling up his property in Levisham. One of the items in the sale notice reads as follows : "There are extensive Beds of Iron Ore under the Commons and as the latter adjoin the Railway for 4 miles, there is every facility for vending the Ore." This sentence must have attracted the attention of James Walker, a Leeds industrialist with an eye for what looked like a good investment. He bought the Manor, and moved with his family from Leeds to Levisham Hall.

The Age of Industry

A few years earlier, the Great Exhibition of 1851 had celebrated the supremacy of British manufacturing prowess. The Yorkshire Gazette boasted : "England has the confidence of the whole world...". There seemed to be nothing that English enterprise and industry could not produce!

LEVISHAM, NEAR PICKERING,
In the North Riding of Yorkshire.
MANOR, ADVOWSON, FARMS, AND LANDS.
TO BE SOLD BY AUCTION,
(IN LOTS,)
By Mr. W. DOBSON,
By order of Assignees of the Rev. ROBERT SKELTON, at the BLACK SWAN INN, in Pickering, on THURSDAY, the 7th of February, 1856, at ONE o'Clock in the Afternoon, subject to such Conditions as shall be then produced,

ALL that the MANOR of LEVISHAM, with its Rights, Royalties, Members, and Appurtenances, extending over 1700 Acres of Commons, Moors, and Wastes.

The ADVOWSON in Fee of the Rectory of Levisham. The Tithes are commuted at £85 6s. 4d.; the Glebe Lands consist of 102A. 1R. 2P.; total Annual Income £200; Population 152; age of present Incumbent 64.

A Capital MESSUAGE, OUTBUILDINGS, and GARDEN, fit for the residence of a respectable Family; and several Messuages, Cottages, Farms, Lands, and Woodlands, containing altogether about 165 Acres in Levisham and Pickering.

The FREESTONE QUARRY on the Common, which adjoins the Whitby and Pickering Railway, with Three Cottages for Labourers, is let to a highly respectable Tenant, at the Annual Rent of £50.

There are extensive Beds of Iron Ore under the Commons and as the latter adjoin the Railway for 4 Miles, there is every facility for vending the Ore.

The Soil is good and productive Barley, Wheat, Turnips, and Seed Land; good Limestone, easy to work, upon the Estate.

Levisham Station on the Whitby and Pickering Railway, admits of easy access to Pickering, Whitby, York, and Scarborough, it being only 6 Miles from Pickering, and 15 from Whitby.

Possession will be given on the Sixth of April next.

Printed Particulars of the several Lots may be had on application to Mr. W. DOBSON, the Auctioneer, Pickering; Mr. PETERS, Solicitor, York; Messrs. WALKER and SON, Solicitors, Malton; Messrs. WALKER and HUNTER, Whitby; Messrs. DONNER and WOODALL, Scarborough; Mr. KENDALL, Solicitor, Pickering; and at the Office of Mr. WATSON,
Pickering 14th Jan., 1856.   In Pickering.

There was unlimited demand for manufactured goods, for the machinery to make them and for railways to transport them - all things English industry could supply, and all needing iron. Not surprising therefore that an ambitious entrepreneur with available capital should see possibilities in the Levisham iron deposits.The Cleveland Hills had long been known as sources of ironstone. An iron bloomery has been excavated on Levisham Moor dating from the

Levisham Hall in the time of Mr & Mrs Barnes Winebush, around 1900.

Roman period[1], as well as the remains of iron workings from the middle ages when iron was also mined in Glaisdale, in the Danby area, and in Bilsdale. The iron working that started up in Glaisdale, Grosmont and Rosedale during the 1850's and 60's was the renewal of an industry with a long past. Walker's plan for an iron works in Levisham recalls the iron-forge in Levisham woods for which successive Lords of Levisham Manor paid 2s annual rent from the 14th to the 17th century, claiming the right to burn charcoal for smelting "from time immemorial"[2].

James Walker, entrepreneur.

There is no doubt that Walker was both enterprising and ambitious. His daughters tell us that he was the eldest son of a Leeds cloth manufacturer, born in 1816, whose family made much of him and gave credence to predictions of what great things he would do in his life:

We always heard in our childhood about some "Predictions" made about our father when quite a baby; they were written down by whoever foretold the future of the child's life, and great things were to be done in it. His mother believed every word of them.

He created the prosperous Leeds textile firm of William Walker & Sons, later called James Walker and then Walker Brothers. They supplied scarlet cloth used in the decor of the Crystal Palace for the Great Exhibition, for which the firm was awarded a Bronze Medal, and various fabrics made by his company were exhibited there. James Walker was on the Leeds Committee for the Exhibition. Early in the morning on the day before the opening, he was at the Crystal Palace supervising the laying of the scarlet cloth when he met the

Prince Consort on an unannounced visit to see how the preparations were going. The next day he and his wife were there in a good position not far from the Duke of Wellington for the State Opening ceremony.

Walker's Pit in Levisham

Having made his mark in the world of textiles, Walker was looking for ways of diversification when the sale of Skelton's estate with the "extensive Beds of Iron Ore under the Commons" offered new opportunities. Unfortunately, he did not have the benefit of a geological survey of the moors made about 30 years later which showed that the ironstone near Levisham was not of a good enough quality to be worth extracting.

The site of his pit is now covered by Forestry Commission plantations and very little of the iron working remains to be seen. Stone dug from a quarry on the slope down into Newtondale below Skelton's Tower was used to construct a 50-foot high chimney, a boiler-house, and a platform alongside the siding to the railway. A shaft was sunk to a depth of over 230 feet. Walker borrowed £2,000 to finance his initial prospecting; in 1861 he borrowed a further £1500. Two years later he had still not found anything worth while, but was still hoping and negotiated for another loan of £3,000[3]. By 1866 he was forced to recognise that the problem was not one that could be solved by more investment. He was facing failure. In a few brief sentences his daughters cover what must have been a traumatic period as their father struggled to keep this calamitous venture going before finally admitting defeat.

In the year 1866 there was much difficulty at my father's ironstone works. The breaking of machinery, water, and other mishaps caused delay and gave great anxiety to my father and mother.

Much money was expended and years of hard work brought no return, and in the end the pit had to be closed down, and we left Levisham.

This was the end of Walker's pit. The chimney was still standing into the 1950's when in the interests of safety it was demolished and the stone used to fill in the pit.

The Walker family

The Walkers' books depict a family typifying what we have come to think of as "Victorian family values" - industrious, devout, given to good works. James was the patriarchal head of the family, uncritically revered by wife and children:

(James) took the lead, physically strong as well as morally. His wife said of him : "The most upright man she had ever come across."

In 1850 he had married Elizabeth Cole who came from a Bradford family with deep roots in the Baptist tradition. Elizabeth Walker comes across as a woman of strong character, high principles and great charm . She accepted a change that she found hard, from the life she was used to in the urban society of West Yorkshire to this remote, tiny village, and established a place for herself in her new community:

Our father had bought an estate with the intention of sinking for ironstone in the Cleveland Hills, and we went to live in the remote moorland village of Levisham.....away from all my mother's relatives and friends, which was a most painful separation to her at first. Her strength of character and beauty of disposition enabled my mother to overcome deprivations and difficulties that would have daunted most people.

One difficulty she shared with many Victorian wives - the burden of repeated childbearing, continuing even after the loss of two babies. Elizabeth Walker came to Levisham with four small children, Francis and Edward aged 5 and 4, Henrietta who was 2 and baby Charles James. During the 10 years that she lived in Levisham, she bore five more children, Janet (b.1859) and Beatrice Mary (b.1861) who both survived, and three babies who died in infancy - Catherine (d 1857), Eleanor (d 1862) and Charlotte Elizabeth,(d 1867). Elizabeth herself died shortly after this last birth, at the age of 39. She was remembered by her daughters as a vivacious, glowing personality :

As I see her in my mind's eye, tall and straight, with lovely brown eyes and bright-coloured hair, light of step and clear of voice, I can hear her ringing laugh as she joined us in our games; they were always so much more enjoyed when she did - there could be no disputes between us then, as there were at other times, for we were strong-willed children.

The Rector, Robert Skelton, was a widower living some way from the centre of the village down by the station. Mrs Walker, reared in a tradition of Christian faith expressed in good works, stepped into a position that combined something of the role of Rector's wife with Lady of the Manor:

On Sunday afternoons the boys and girls of the village came to our house. Before her marriage my mother had helped a good deal in the work of Sunday Schoools, and so she began at once in her own home to carry on the same kind of classes. A pleasant room was filled with them and us children, who all listened full of attention to her beautiful way of telling Bible Stories, and we sang all our childish hymns with delight.

In the summer, the young men of the village came one night a week . My mother would take temperance, manliness, and other helpful subjects to talk to them upon, as they sat round her in the garden, and some of them, living today, tell of the influence the remembrance of her words had upon them all their lives. She ordered periodicals from London. and when they came we distributed them in the village. Once I was stopped by an old shepherd who said, "Let me look at Dickie Cobden." He evidently knew something about the Corn Laws agitation.

Another evening in the week the elder girls came, which was a most happy time to them. They were shown how to make pretty things and taught to do fine needlework. They loved to be with her. In every house patchwork quilts were made, and quilted, ready for when the girls married....

Perhaps her early death helped to impress her memory upon all, and made them realise what a privilege it had been to be associated with her. The whole village mourned her, and it was said, "She could not have done more good even if she had lived longer"..We heard this years after she died.

James Walker was a sterner figure. Brought up to be admired and respected, he expected unquestioning obedience from his children:

Once my father had an attack of lumbago on a Sunday, and as he was not able to go to Church with us, we had to go by ourselves. It was a very hot day, and we did not want to go, so we wasted the time, and then went back home, and up to father's room to tell him, the bells had stopped, thinking that was reason enough for not going on. But he did not think so, and in firm tones, said, "Go back at once", and the whole six of us had to walk up Lockton hill again and go in disgracefully late to the service.

A revealing little story is told by Janet when she was looking after her father at the end of his life :

A day or two before father passed on, 30th September 1894, I was sitting with him. He was then seventy eight years old; time had not dimmed his eye or memory. Quietly he spoke: "I can't bear to think I am leaving you three unprovided for". He smiled when I said that it did not matter. "Ah! but I made a mistake". He had had a great opportunity of success with his gas patent which had taken much work to arrive at, and it slipped through his fingers. I was sitting mending his socks, a very rare thing to be in his room, dreaming a little dream, and it startled me to hear him own he had made a mistake. "Now", I said, "because you have said that we will never reproach your memory", and we never have.

Here was a man who was not used to admitting ever making a mistake - his daughter was startled to hear him! It was a failure as a businessman that he admitted to, a failure to take an opportunity which would have left his daughters financially secure: that was how he saw his duty as a father.

Levisham in the Walkers' time

A large part of the interest in the Walkers' writings is in their anecdotes about Levisham life and characters. The period when they were living in Levisham is in one sense well-documented: the ten-yearly Census returns, Parish Registers, a variety of documents supplying names and factual information about people and events in the village. The Walker sisters put flesh

Levisham Church, from Lockton Bank.

onto dry bones, bringing to life some of the village characters, conveying an impression of the atmosphere of Levisham life. In spite of the unhappy events that overshadowed their years at Levisham, their recollections are full of affection. They remember sights and sounds, details that stick in the minds of children. Their anecdotes ramble inconsequentially here and there, touching on places, people, events. Sometimes the facts are wrong -

Levisham beck is shallow as seen at the mill; it runs over a bed of smooth stones and pebbles of many colours to be seen beneath the clean water, rippling with a happy sound as it flows through the mill meadows before it races on to reach the River Esk and join the North Sea.. - (in fact, Levisham beck flows south to join the Derwent).

The language is sometimes flowery :

It is a joyous way to walk along the bank in summer time on the side where ox-eye daisies, blue speedwells and purple orchises glow in the tall grass.... - the details they recall, mundane :

A plank is thrown across it with a light hand rail, for the beck becomes swollen after heavy rains and overflows its banks, and the Valley Church of Saint Mary can be reached by those who come from Lockton to worship there, instead of going by the road past the mill....

but they are remembering the vivid impressions of a childhood spent in a place they came to love.

Home life

Some of their recollections are about their own home and family :

Our house had a well I remember. We were not allowed tea. Oatmeal porridge ground at the mill, made with milk, was our breakfast dish, and when we went to school to Thorner and the other girls told us of their meals, tea and toast and marmalade, they laughed at ours, theirs sounded so much superior. I remember seeing the 'green' tea being mixed with the black; they were in different quantities and the sugar pincers used to cut the sugar loaf into pieces. And on Saturdays when Old Hannah finished up she would take the long brush and sweep across the row of bells high up near the roof of the kitchen that they jangled in protest. Tables were scrubbed so white.....

One of our little pleasures was the way birthdays were kept. The one whose day it was going to be had to go to bed early the night before, so that presents could be wrapped up and messages written, which helped to make the others feel important too in doing it. Then there was something to eat suitable to the time of year. In September Orleans plums were ripe, and a delicious compote of these and whipped cream served in custard glasses was the treat. In November it was parkin, and the bonfire celebration for one of my brothers; another had a party in the hay-field, and in early Spring it was toffee for a sister, and rook-shooting for two others. These were real festivals in our childhood.

The Prince Consort died on the 14th of December, 1861. I remember going to Church with mamma. She wore a dress of a beautiful purple colour, with a black silk mantle and bonnet; my royal mourning I do not recollect. The whole country was in great sorrow at this sudden calamity.

The Prince of Wales was married on the 10th of March, 1863, to a Danish Princess. They were later King Edward VIII the Peace Maker and Queen Alexandra the Beloved.

When our father and mother were both away some of the villagers came to ask us for "material". They wanted a flag for the village. The friend who was taking care of us found some red, white and blue pieces in the house, and the tailor took them and made a flag, which they hoisted at the end of a high building, and I can remember the great pleasure with which we saw it floating in the air. I still have the medal that was struck to commemorate this wedding; the two faces in profile surmounted with the Prince of Wales' Feathers, and motto, "Ich Dien", and below oak leaves and acorns entwined, with the words "May they be happy."

A great delight on a wild morning, wind blowing, and perhaps rain falling, was to rush down the back stairs and out of doors into the garden to gather up pears and apples that strewed the ground, and back again to bed to eat them. Then there were some plum trees that grew above a bed of mint. The fragrant scent of bruised mint will yet recall to us the taste of the delicious ripe purple plums that fell into it.....

There was a fig-tree nailed to the wall, and the fruit hidden under the dark-green leaves, was luscious and juicy. At the far end of the garden was the rookery. In the Spring, when the rooks were building their nests, and busily flying with long twigs and wisps of straw in their beaks, we children would sit in the window-seat watching them with delight. It was a wonderful garden to play hide-and-seek in; there were some fine old trees as well as the shrubbery, a great place also for the birds to nest in. Then on higher ground there was the old white summer-house, a most happy place to play in, covered with honeysuckle.....

Another delight was to climb a high wall on which fruit ripened lusciously, and run along the top of it. We did it once too often. Our baby brother was with us that day - we ran to the end and left him. There was a scream - he had fallen off into the orchard on the other side. he was picked up white and still, and when the doctor, who had to be sent for from miles away, came, and shook his head, we thought we should never be happy again. It was feared the spine was injured, but he grew up straight and strong of limb.

Village personalities

There are a number of anecdotes about village people.

In our village there were some very interesting characters. One known to us all as "Old Hannah" told me how in her girlhood they were frightened when they saw the "red-coats" come, as they feared husbands, fathers and sons might be taken away to be soldiers in the War. She was remembering Waterloo. ...

"Old Hannah", who in her youth had been a servant at a lonely moorland inn, also remembered how Press Gangs impressed men into the Naval Service. Then the first time she ever went in a train (to Whitby) she was so terrified that she lay down flat on the floor and moaned.

The railway through Newton Dale was one of the first in the country, engineered by George Stephenson and opened in 1836, originally using horse-drawn carriages then converted to steam in 1847. There were naturally mistakes and accidents in the development of such a revolutionary new mode of transport :

At that time there was a steep gradient on the line and the train had to be lowered down gradually. A steel rope was used, and I remember hearing how this once broke. There was a serious accident at Beckhole down this incline,

WHITBY & PICKERING RAILWAY.

GREAT ACCOMMODATION TO THE PUBLIC.

CHEAP, SAFE, AND EXPEDITIOUS TRAVELLING. Twice Every Day, (except Sundays,) between WHITBY AND PICKERING ; and Once Every Day, (Sundays excepted), between those Places and York, Hull, Wakefield, Sheffield, Huddersfield, Halifax, Manchester, Birmingham, and the rest of the Kingdom.

A Railway Coach leaves Whitby for Pickering at Half-Past SIX o'Clock in the Morning, and in the Evening at Half-Past FIVE ; and Pickering, for Whitby, Every Morning at Half-Past TEN o'Clock, and in the Evening, after the Arrival of the York Coach, about Half-Past FIVE o'Clock.

The Coach leaves Pickering for York at NINE o'Clock in the Morning, and York for Pickering at TWO in the Afternoon.

Fare from Whitby to Pickering 3s. 6d., 3s., and 2s. 6d.
——————— Pickering to York 10s. and 6s.

Yorkshire Gazette, 1836.

and two or three people were killed. After this the rails were taken up a considerable distance and a " deviation" was made.

A notable figure in the Village was the Postman. He walked every day from the Post Office, six miles away across the valley, which meant coming down a very steep hill and walking up another. As soon as he reached the top he blew a horn for it to be known he had come, and letters must be ready for him to take back. This was the only way of posting letters at that time in the Village. There was neither Pillar Box nor Post Office. There were very few letters to deliver, except the daily call at our house with the letter bag. Every Friday there was a pasty waiting, placed at the end of the dresser, and one of us liked, if we were allowed, to give it to the postman. Telegrams cost six shillings to be delivered, the charge being at that time a shilling a mile from the Post Office to the receiver

One of the aristocrats of the Village was Miles Close. He got across his brother-in-law, the Squire-Rector, who lived in Levisham Hall before us. There was a direct view from the upper windows of the house down the valley to Farworth.[Farwath]. To annoy him Mr Close planted a row of Scots Pines. In a few years these grew into beautiful trees. Our mother loved to look at them, and she said how strange it was that such an act should give her so much pleasure.

He had one son, John Close, who never married, but he was an authority in the Village life, being rich, and he was also a Churchwarden, and looked after the Church rates and tithes. When we knew him he was wearing up his father's clothes - a long dark, green swallow-tailed coat, Regency cut, and knee breeches with closely brass-buttoned gaiters.

The mother of Mr Dixon was a very strong, active woman, who kept the inn, 'The Horse Shoe'. She wore very short skirts and pattens, a white mob cap, with an old black bonnet on top of it, and had a very gruff voice. She was always spoken of as Mary Dixon.

It was an old-world inn with the thickly sanded floor that crunched under your feet, and there were long churchwarden pipes leaning against the mantlepiece, and spittoons on each side of the fireplace. There was no shop in the village. The inn was the only place where anything could be bought. I remember particularly she sold peppermints and matches and, I believe, tobacco. I do not remember anything more. Mrs. Dixon was not a good manager. A story told in the village was that one day she went to borrow a loaf of bread at one of the farms. 'The wreets are coming today,' she said,'and I have not any bread in the house to give them'. Journeymen wheelwrights came from the next village to mend farm implements from time to time, and she had to have some food ready for them.

She was active in mind as well as body , and knew the affairs of most people as well as her own.

Mamma sent me on messages into the village and trusted me to carry delicacies made for the miller, who was very ill and only cared to eat what our mother sent him by me. I walked down the steep hill where cows were cropping the bright green grass between the furze bushes.....The mill once reached I was happy in telling what I had come for, and having a skip round looking at the mill hoist lowering bags of flour, and the men dusty and white carrying sacks of grain on their backs or helping the farmer to load the waggon waiting for flour and oatmeal, which had been ground from wheat and oats grown in his own fields, by the massive millstones the great wooden water wheel turned, moved by the water passing over it. Sometimes there was no "humming" sound, the wheel was "dry", no water to turn it. Or there were the hens pecking up the corn scattered around, and ducklings like little balls of yellow fluff......Then came the climb up the hill back home, but the basket was lighter now....Kind Mrs. Russell's face I can see clearly; she did not let me seee her husband, he was ill a long time - a "decline" it was called.

The name of Hesele Newton was another in the village who was ill a long time also. It was such an attractive house to us from the outside, the windows seemed church-like, pointed frame and lattice of leaded glass panes. It was a homely well-to-do farmhouse, many sons and daughters grew up there, and I can remember their mother with a brown sunburnt face and broad smile of welcome when in later years we went to spend holidays in Levisham, always dressed in black and a large straw hat on her head. She had the bringing up of that family of boys and girls alone, another one of the great company of mothers who have sent out their children to face life bravely by their example and teaching. Her

Levisham Mill with turf stack outside.

daughter Grace we never forgot. She made our mourning when mamma died and our little black frocks and jackets went to London first and then on to Nova Scotia, fashioned by her skilful fingers.....

One of the boys in the village, a farmer's nephew, was quite a hero. He was a sailor on a whale boat, and once when he came back I had been sent into the village with a message. It was the farm-men's dinner hour; they were gathered round him resting and listening to his tales of the sea. As I passed by I overheard him say he had been to Greenland. I did not know where this place was and thought it must be a long way off. He must have been employed in the whale fishery. At that time Whitby was a centre for this industry, and blubber, of which train-oil is made, and the firm elastic substance taken from the upper jaw of the whale, known as whalebone were valuable. It was profitable work, but the taking of whales was highly dangerous to the whalemen.

Church & Chapel

Religion flourished in Victorian times, both Church of England and non-conformity. Sometimes they operated as rivals, but in Levisham Church and Chapel seem to have co-existed harmoniously, for example Matthew Dixon, one of the principal farmers in the mid-century, was Churchwarden in 1846; in 1865 he was the Society Steward at the Primitive Methodist Chapel. Church practices change over the years. In the 18th and early 19th centuries celebration of the Holy Communion was infrequent - three times a year at Levisham in 1764[4]. A century later under the influence of the Oxford Movement more frequent communions became customary - at Levisham, four or five times a year as well as the great festivals. John Close displays the innate conservatism of those who always prefer to keep to the old traditions :

There was another wealthy farmer who was always spoken of as Mat Dixon. He was not so much connected with the Church as Mr Close was. From very ancient times there had been a Chapel of Ease for the Village, to be used in Winter to save the walk down the steep hill to the lonely Parish Church of St Mary in the valley. This fell into ruin and decay, and the building not being repaired the furnishings were scattered. The wooden pulpit was found in an outbuilding, and the Font, which is supposed to be of Saxon origin, of roughly-hewn stone, bears a cross and rope ornamentation on it. This was found in Mr Mat Dixon's farmyard, being used as a cattle-trough. When the Chapel of Ease was restored in 1894, the Chapel entirely rebuilt on the old site, was consecrated as Christ Church, by the Archbishop of York, Dr. Maclagan, and the Font was brought back and put into its right postition and use.

One summer, when we were re-visiting our old home, we stayed on the Sunday morning to the service of Holy Communion after Morning Prayer. Meeting him [John Close] later, he said to us : "I should have like to have spoken to you, but you stopped Church", which was his way of expressing "the Eucharist". He only partook of the Sacrament, as he called it, three times a year.

In 1859 a small Primitive Methodist Chapel was built in the village, and earnest workers and fervent members attended Church at one time and Chapel at another, as services were arranged alternately. Miss Lightowler was the "Tract Distributor," sent out from this Chapel. She was the daughter of the old Schoolmaster. Once a year the congregation celebrated the Anniversary of the opening of the Chapel. There were special preachers on the Sunday, and the next

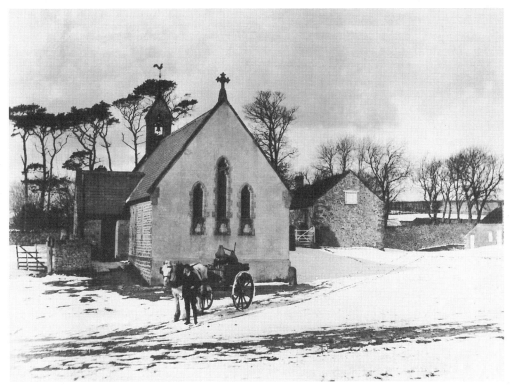

The Chapel of Ease, rebuilt 1894, now Levisham Parish Church.

day "the tea-feast" was held in the Chapel, and lemon-cheese cakes and curd-cheese cakes and good tea and rich cream was enjoyed by everyone. Then a public meeting was held in Mr.Dixon's big barn, and recitations, speeches and hymn-singing ended the day.

In summer the members of all the Chapels around had what was called a "Camp Meeting," held at a place named Stape, on the Moors. It was a revival, and many hymns were sung. One was "My Barque is bound for Heaven, on Time's wild restless flood." I was told of it by Old Hannah. and I thought it meant really sailing in a ship to Heaven.

*We went to Lockton Church service on Sunday afternoons. The Vicar stood in the reading desk, with Mr Hoggard, the parish clerk, below him to say A-a-men. When the prayers were ended, the clerk walked down the aisle with a large Paslm Book, bound in brown leather under his arm, to the little song gallery at the west end, where the musicians sat who played a trombone, a bassoon and a clarionet. He then opened the large book and said, "Let us sing to the praise and glory of God, part of the 9th Psalm," or it might be "Let us sing to the praise and glory of God, part of 'The Evening Hymn,'" and then read aloud the first four lines of "Glory to Thee, my God this night," which was **the** Evening Hymn at that time.*

Sermons were long, and pews were straight and narrow, with hard seats, so we were glad when the singing began. Two little sisters were buried in the churchyard, and we used to go round and look at their graves after service.

Special Occasions

Every year early in July the Friendly Society - the Order of Shepherds, held a meeting, which was called "The Club Feast." It was a great time for all, grown-ups and children. Friends came from a distance to see their relations, who had made all sorts of good things to eat, and the village street was made tidy, the geese were cooped up that day, and the horses kept in their stables. Stalls were set up on the green with every kind of attraction to childish eyes, toys and ginger-bread, nuts and oranges....

There was a service in the Valley Church. The members walked in procession two-and-two, carrying their crooks and wearing their badge of association. Once one of my sisters was staying in Levisham at the time, and wished to go to the service. Besides the Rector's daughter, who played the harmonium, she was the only girl present.

The little Church was full of men, who sang "All people that on earth do dwell" with real devotion. ....The procession was re-formed to walk back to the village for dinner. She saw one young man break the ranks and stand by our mother's grave with his hat off, reading the inscription. "Did you know my mother?" she asked. He said at once, " She was the best friend I ever had," adding, "I am over from America where my home now is, and I have come to be present at this Club Feast specially, and to pay tribute to her memory."

[Village people] tell of an old celebration of the harvest home which is very ancient called the "Mell". When the last sheaf of corn is cut, a plentiful supper is made for the harvesters, the last day of reaping is known as "Mell Day". It was a great feast. When the last handful is bound up in the golden sheaf the sheaves are all placed upright in lots of ten or twelve each called stooks, the farmer's head man or some other elderly person employed during the harvest, proceeds in a loud voice to "Shout the mell", which is celebrated in the following rhyme :

> *"Blest the day that Christ was born*
> *We've gett'n mell of Mr. Newton's corn*
> *Weel bound and better shorn,*
> *Hip! Hip! Hip! Huzza! Huzza!"*

"Our last Mell was between forty and fifty years since," Mrs. Harland said. "It was a great feast of all kinds of things; they always ate warm currant short cakes well buttered - we called them sad cakes - with hot tea, and finished off with whiskey and smokes. All who had helped were asked and friends were all in too, and songs were sung by the reapers. It was a great time of merriment and festivity." The last mell sheaf was also used in the process of preparing the wheat to be ready for the Christmas dish, making Frumerty, the dry husk of the wheat must be hulled, boiled in milk and seasoned with cinnamon, sugar, or treacle.....

There were many of the old rites and customs of celebrating the harvest home. Another she told me of was the corn image called by many names : harvest queen, harvest doll, corn baby, the emblem of the corn spirit, put on a high pole decorated with grain and flowers, or made from the last sheaf gathered and brought in with the last load from the field with the singing and shouting of the harvesters and later the pole with the wheat was reared up in the stackyard for the birds in winter. Harvest home celebration is very ancient and thought by students of folklore to be the survival of rites originally religious or magical. The belief in witchcraft held sway when we went to Levisham.

When the last load had gone from the harvest field, gleaners were allowed to come and gather up all the farmers had generously left behind, and they took their small sheaves to the miller who dressed it for them, without cost, for their Christmas "Frummerty", which is corn "creed" in the oven in milk and sweetened with treacle and eaten at this festival. Old Nanny Pearson told me it was the custom when eating it to provide two candles and light them on Christmas Eve; a ceremony of "Light" come down from the past.....Usually one candle only was used, and very often none. People went to bed early in those days and had to be careful.

On Christmas morning the village children came quite early and sang "Christians awake, Salute the happy morn!" and wished us a Merry Christmas. A large trayful of spice buns was ready with a new penny on the top for each of them. We had great preparations ourselves for the day : holly and ivy were hung up and wreaths made, and we had a Christmas tree which was really a marvel to those who saw it...

Levisham Village

A Footpath way from the Well was up past the growth of wild rose trees and luscious ripe blackberries which grow there, and prickly whin, to the other side of the steep hill whereon Levisham stands very much alone a village of the moors

Years ago a rich farmer pointed across to it with a scornful finger, saying "See yon? That's Lersum, t'last spot God made - leads nowhere.".....

The layout of the village today has changed little since the Walker's time, but the appearance has changed - thatched roofs have gone, the road is tarred, grass verges kept short by lawnmowers rather than geese. The *"new farmhouse with the blue slates"* is there with its date, 1860, over the front door :

The inn stood at the top of the village and faced down the street; wayfarers coming and going were easily seen by her. The Stackyards and garths were behind the houses; many of them were thatched, the others were tiled except the new farmhouse which had blue slates. There is only the limestone road, which is bordered by slopes of green grass kept short by the geese plucking at it, which goes through the village to the hilltop.

There are no set paths. We usually walked on the road for fear of the geese. An old gander hissing and chasing little bare legs with socks on was alarming.

Even as children, the Walkers were aware of the difference between city life in *"papa's Leeds"* full of shops and amenities and the sparseness of village life.They were acquainted with city people who came to enjoy the beauties of moorland summers and they knew the hardiness needed for living all the year round on the Yorkshire moors:

Once when my little brother and I had gone outside the gate, and he had a small wheelbarrow brightly painted red and blue, a voice said jokingly, "Will you give me your barrow?" Charlie said "You should go to Leeds to buy one." Afterwards I said reprovingly "Charles James, you should not have told Mr. Dixon to go to papa's Leeds!"

I remember one of those misty Autumn mornings which give such an indescribable sensation to one who notices the peculiar charm of an English early change from summer heat; a time when corn has just been gathered in and the whirr of the thrashing machine is heard, giving an idea of prosperity and preparation for a supply of bread, which shall give courage to face the rigours of a Winter.

Those Northern Moors are a dream of beauty in Summer, but when the frost and snow are on them, then let those who live there pile on the turves, and bid defiance to the cold. I remember it all so well, and the people who spent their lives in quiet contentment unknown to the City-born, and yet who read the newspaper and knew of the doings among the great ones of the earth.

The cutting of turves with a mattock for the household fires began in the early part of the year. They were left in piles on the moor all through the summer to dry, then in the autumn, when there was little to be done on the land, the leading began, and the turf-stacks were built up again for winter use. There was the open hearth in most of the homes except ours, an iron-plate with place for the banking up of the squares of turf. Above was the "reckon", a steel bar: it had a hinge, by means of which it could be brought forward to hang a kettle on, or the turf-cake-pan over the fire. This pan was a flat round of iron with a handle over it, and a cover which fitted closely, on which the hot ashes were spread so that the little currant "turf cakes" were baked at the same time above and below. The "Yetling," a three-legged pan, was used for boiling bacon and vegetables, and could stand on the hearth-plate, in the hot ashes, or be hung on the reckon. The "skep" was a flat open basket used to bring the turf into the house.

Levisham village, looking towards the Horseshoe Inn.

A hearth in Levisham with its "reckon"

At this time the Wood Shed was filled for winter use. There were very few coal fires, owing to the expense of leading it from a distance, the railway station being in the Valley two miles away.

The ten years that the Walkers spent in Levisham left a lasting impression on their daughters. They came back for holidays and visited people they had known. Year after year they entered their names in the Visitors' Book in the church. In the churchyard is a memorial stone to Elizabeth Walker and the three daughters who died in infancy; inside the church a memorial tablet :

In Memory of our Father, JAMES WALKER

of Leeds and Levisham, 1816 - 1894,

our Mother ELIZABETH WALKER, 1827 - 1867

and their children, Francis 1865 - 1920

and Henrietta 1854 - 1936,

this tablet is placed here where they worshipped for many years

by Charles James, Janet and Beatrice Mary Walker, September 1936.

"O Ye Spirits and Souls of the Righteous

Bless ye the Lord".

JOHN SKELTON AND THE EVANGELICAL REVIVAL

In 1833, a little pamphlet entitled "The Rector's Son; or Memoirs of Mr.John Skelton, late of Levisham" was printed for the author, John Watson, who had been asked to write " a short narrative of his life", drawing on the Journal kept by John Skelton during his last years. It is a piece of writing in the same style as Memoirs that appeared regularly at that time in the pages of the Methodist Magazine, in which the life of a deceased member was held up as an example for the edification of the readers. Its purpose is explained in its first paragraph - *"to place before us the example......*(so that)*.we may catch the spirit ..."* It is not a "memoir" in the present understanding of the term in that it tells us little about the life of its subject apart from his experiences as an enthusiastic evangelical preacher. Both its content and style provide insight into the spirit of early 19th century Methodism which made a notable impact on contemporary life. By its publication, the author hoped to *"improve"* the death of his friend, that is, to make it the occasion of benefit to its readers through the moral lessons they could learn from it.

Until the 18th century, the Established Church dominated the English religious scene. There had been dissenters ever since the Reformation - in spite of attempts to make the Church of England broad enough to be acceptable to everyone, there were always a few on both the Catholic and Puritan wings who were prepared to accept the penalties of non-conformity,- but only in towns were they likely to be numerous enough to have their own places of worship. In most villages, the Anglican Church had a monopoly on religious practice.

The 18th century was a period when established patterns of work and of social and political organisation were breaking down in the face of industrial and agricultural change, foreign war and threat of political revolution. At times when people feel unusually vulnerable and insecure, the certainties of passionate religious faith have a particular appeal. John Wesley and his followers were the charismatics of their day, and the response up and down the country to their preaching showed how a deep a chord of spiritual longing they touched. Jonathan Ellerby, required as Constable of the little village of Hartoft to send in a return about Non Conformist places of worship in 1828, reported with shaky spelling but unshaking conviction, "wee are seaven of hus joined the Metherdist Connection but has no Chappel so that wherever a raye of Divine Love dartes down upon hus there wee worship God."[5] The Skelton memoir gives us a glimpse of the emotional passion stirred by such evangelical preachers; those who responded to the call to repentance and new faith found themselves caught up in the excitement of a great cosmic drama of salvation .

The Methodist preachers were well versed in the Bible, as can be inferred from the number of biblical quotations and references,as well as the echoes of biblical language in the memoir, all deriving from a familiarity with the scriptures gained by reading the Bible in the way that Skelton did after his conversion - cover to cover, six chapters a day. The clear and compelling theme of mankind doomed to destruction unless saved by Christ was not only expounded in preaching but set to music and sung in the hymns that were a feature of Methodist gatherings. The writer of the Memoir intersperses his text with verses of hymns which would be familiar to his readers.

The aim of the evangelist was to bring his hearers to a sense of their own guilt. This was more than intellectual assent to the notion of sinfulness; feeling was important to prepare the way for a readiness to respond with relief to the offer of salvation - *"Mr Skelton had no notion of a religion without feeling; his first object was to make people feel their guilt and danger as sinners; and then he exhorted them to rest not till they felt the love of God...."* After the " *conviction of sin"* and the repentance leading to a felt sense of salvation, came the third stage of *sanctification* as the *justified* individual devoted his/her life to the service of God. In reading the account of the *"extraordinary revival"*, of the *"souls set at liberty"*, we can sense something of the atmosphere of energy and excitement that brought colour and drama into the lives of the participants.

Skelton's initial conversion experience, we are told, was in 1821 at a lovefeast at a Wesleyan chapel. There was a Wesleyan chapel in Hungate, Pickering from 1812 which could have been where this took place. In Lockton[6], a Wesleyan Society had been formed as early as 1797 with 5 members, and by 1818 they were using a house registered as a meeting place, but their first chapel was not built till 1822. The lovefeast[7] was something Wesley had met early in his career during his contact with the Moravians. It was, he said, "celebrated in so decent and solemn a manner as a Christian of the apostolic age would have allowed to be worthy of Christ"[8], and he later introduced it into the Methodist Societies. It was an occasion for "free and familiar conversation in which every man, yea, and every woman, has liberty to speak whatever may be to the glory of God." Going back in origin to the "agape" of the early church which seems to have been a varient on the Lord's Supper, in Methodist usage the sharing of food (usually cake or a bun), and drink (water or tea passed round in a two-handled mug), was the focal point of a service of hymns, prayer, exhortation and testimonies, a time of intense religious fellowship which was likely to inspire heightened emotion and so was often the occasion for conversions. At a time when there were few public entertainments, lovefeasts became popular - "more popular than any other of our peculiar church privileges.....many have been known to apply quarter after quarter for admission", "the most popular and exciting of our social meetings", so had to be carefully regulated . The excesses that could occur are implied behind a suggested 10-point scheme for regulating love feasts - no "improper persons" should be present, only members of the society, or "other serious persons" who normally had to be specially invited; there should be no "wild irregularities"; never more than one person speaking at a time, no-one to speak without the permission of the presiding Preacher. "Testimonies" featured not only in lovefeasts but in the week by week meetings of the bands into which all Methodist societies were divided, when they encouraged each other by sharing their experiences. In this way all members gained a sense of their own significance. They were not just passive recipients of the ministrations of others, but all had an active part to play in the spiritual life of the society.

Lay participation was one of the key features of Methodist organisation. The Plan for Travelling & Local Preachers in the Pickering Circuit 1831-2 shows 21 chapels holding weekly services with 2 ordained ministers (Travelling Preachers) and 18 Local Preachers to man them. The memoir tells that after his conversion experience, John Skelton's family *"wished him to become a clergyman of the established church"*, following in the footsteps of his father and older brother, but that instead *"he was proposed and accepted as a Local Preacher"*. His name does not appear on any of the Circuit Plans so far found covering this period. Usually a Local Preacher operated within his own Circuit. The Pickering Circuit in 1831 covered a wide area taking in Kirbymoorside, Nunnington, Farndale, Gillimore (sic), Rosedale, and eastwards to Wilton and Ebberston - large distances for preachers to cover, even when geography was taken into account in the planning. Skelton travelled widely, *"not only in the villages of his own neighbourhood, but also in the Malton, Whitby and other Circuits"*, and *"Stockton, York, Knaresborough, Whitby, Robin Hood's Bay, Glazedale, Fryup, Harrogate, Green Hammerton, etc"* are all mentioned as *"scenes of labour"*. His friends believed that the exertion of this ceaseless travelling contributed to his early death.

The progress of Methodism was an up-and-down affair. A surge of enthusiasm would inflame a particular village or district; new members flocked in, the society rejoiced - and perhaps built or enlarged a chapel. Then the fervour died down, there was discouragement, talk of "backsliders", and much earnest preaching and praying for a revival. Skelton's conversion in the spring of 1821 was during one of these times of "revival" which had started in Lastingham. According to an article in the Methodist Magazine, "It has pleased God graciously to revive his work in several villages in this Circuit, so that our Societies.....have been more than doubled in 3 or 4 places......The subjects of this work consist of persons of all ages, and almost all descriptions of character..."

Sometime later, *"Mr Skelton was rather discouraged on account of the prayer-meetings being so thinly attended"*, but he did not give in, and *"a glorious work broke out in Lockton...."*, an *"extraordinary revival"*, which *"produced a strong sensation in the neighbourhood...."*. one wonders what the sensations were of John's brother Robert, Rector of the next village. Did he feel this was poaching on his patch? Was he embarrassed by his brother's involvement with a rival religious organisation? There is no indication in the memoir. Robert wrote a letter to a friend after John's death couched in terms of conventional piety that does not give any hint of a breach between them, but it is noticeable that there is no monumental inscription to John amongst all the Skelton memorials in Levisham church.

John Wesley had not intended to break with the Church of England. He understood his mission as the renewal of the church of which he was a priest, and to the end of his life saw his followers as societies within that church, not a separate sect, and even when a separation had taken place and rivalry grew up there was never the same animosity as was still widely felt towards the Catholic church. Contemporary attitudes towards Roman Catholicism are illustrated in the account of Skelton's conversion of a *"poor papist devotee"* ; the words from his Journal about this Catholic convert, *"the man of sin, the son of perdition, whose coming is after the working of Satan...."* are loaded with an intense hostility that reflects the common attitude of his day.

The movement of which John Skelton was an enthusiastic early exponent took root in the area of the North Yorkshire Moors, finding particular support in villages where the established Church was weak, either because of the poor quality of the incumbent or because there was no incumbent living in the village. Two neighbouring villages to Levisham, Lockton and Newton-on-Rawcliffe, were Chapelries of larger parishes, Lockton of Middleton, Newton of

Pickering, so did not have a resident clergyman and in both villages Methodist chapels, Wesleyan and Primitive, were established early and were well supported. In Levisham which always had a resident Rector, Methodism came late and seems to have been less influential. There is no record of a Methodist Society there till 1842 when the Primitive Circuit Preachers' Plan shows a meeting in Levisham alternate Sundays and a weeknight meeting once a month on a Monday. The Chapel was built in 1859, and the Plan for 1865 records services held every Sunday evening with an additional afternoon service alternate weeks and a fortnightly weeknight meeting. At that date one of the principal farmers in the village, Matthew Dixon, was the Society Steward and Levisham provided one Local Preacher, John Jackson, a farm labourer.

A dispassionate estimate of the strengths and weaknesses of Methodism in the northern area of the moors is given by Canon Atkinson, Vicar of Danby from 1847 to 1900. He describes his first visit to the parish where he was to serve for so long. He met his predecessor in his squalid home, and was taken by him to the church of which he was the " reverend but hardly reverent minister " where Atkinson was shocked by the shabby, uncared-for state of what he saw - the dirt, negligence, slovenliness of it all. He comments: " I could well understand how the only religious life in the district should be among and due to the exertions of the Wesleyan and Primitive Methodists", and he appreciated the advice of his patron who had written to him when he accepted the incumbency, "You will find the Wesleyans worthy of much consideration. Indeed I think that if it had not been for them and their influence religion would have practically died altogether out in these Dales".[9]

The Skelton Family

The reader who goes to this memoir hoping for interesting details of John Skelton's personal life will be disappointed. Skelton Tower, standing out on the skyline above Newtondale, and the array of Skelton memorials in St Mary's Church indicate a family of considerable consequence whom we should like to know more about. On the the title page John Skelton is called "The Rector's Son"; later, his brother has become Rector; we learn that he was born in Levisham in 1793 and died and was buried there in 1831, and that is about all! Fuller in-formation about his family has to be sought elsewhere.

John's father, Robert Skelton sr, came to Levisham as the new Rector in 1786.

He was 27 years old, the only son of a yeoman farmer from the village of Aislaby near Middleton, about eight miles from Levisham. He was growing up there during the early

Skelton Tower.

years of the Methodist revival. When John Wesley came to the Pickering area in 1766, Middleton was a parish where he was welcomed by the Rector and invited to preach in the Parish Church where, he recorded in his Journal, "all the congregation seemed earnest to know how they might worship God in spirit and in truth ." Robert Skelton, then a boy of 7, could have been amongst that congregation. His outlook would be likely to be affected by his parish priest, and the Rev. John King who was rector of Middleton until 1782 was known throughout the area both as a popular preacher and as a supporter and persuasive advocate of the evangelical cause.[10]

Skelton was ordained a Deacon in the Anglican Church in 1781 in Gloucester. Nothing has been discovered as to what took him there, nor what he did for the next two years, but in 1783 his father died and he inherited a house together with "all my lands or parcels of land wheresoever situated", the phraseology suggesting quite a lot of property. He was appointed to the Perpetual Curacy of Rosedale on the nomination of "the principal inhabitants". Three years later the Rectory of Levisham fell vacant, and Skelton was able to secure this appointment in addition to the Rosedale curacy.

In 1787 he married Sarah, daughter of John Watson, one of the principal farmers of Rosedale. The events of their family life can be traced in the Levisham Parish Registers and monumental inscriptions in St Mary's Church. They had three children, Sarah born 1788, Robert 1791 and John in 1793. They all spent the rest of their lives in Levisham. Sarah married Miles Close of Brompton, near Northallerton who became one of the chief farmers in the village and a pillar of the community, serving for years in the various offices of Churchwarden, Overseer of the Poor, Constable; Robert, the elder son and heir, followed his father as Rector and Lord of the Manor and brought up his large family there; John, who did not marry, continued to live in the family home until his death at the age of 37 in 1831. For almost a century from the time of the first Robert's arrival as Rector to the death of the second Robert in 1877, the Skeltons were the leading family in the village.

Skelton came to Levisham during the period of agricultural revolution, when long-established farming practices were being replaced by methods that were potentially more profitable for those with capital and initiative. In Levisham, the Enclosure of the Open Fields in 1770 had freed the arable land of the village from the constraints of old restrictive customs, making farm land an attractive investment. Skelton soon began acquiring land and property in the parish starting with a tenanted farm in 1788, buying other properties when they came on the market. His biggest acquisition was the purchase of the Manor of Levisham in 1792 which included the "newly erected messuage or Mansion House", Levisham Hall, and extensive land. Robert jr and John were joint heirs of their father's considerable estate, so after his death in 1818 both were men of substance.

One of Robert sr's projects as Rector was to rebuild the Parish Church of St Mary's which stands in the valley between the villages of Lockton and Levisham - a reconstruction so complete that almost no trace of the medieval building remained. A family vault for the Rector's family was created within the altar rails and over the years the memorials to family members underlined their status in the community.

The references in 'The Rector's Son' to John Skelton's childhood "under the influence of divine impressions", influenced by "a pious female , who was an

Inside St. Mary's Church, showing some of the Skelton Memorial tablets.

inmate in the family" suggest a family life within the evangelical tradition, with the "vanities by which he was surrounded" and the" sinning and repenting" which are described in the Memoir not so much objective realities as part of the scenario which formed the backdrop to evangelical preaching, the darkness of the unredeemed life painted blackly in contrast to the bright new post-conversion character.

The Family of Robert Skelton jr

John's brother Robert was Rector of Levisham until the end of his life. In 1816 he had married Jane Richardson of Thornton Dale who was connected with the well-to-do Lockton family of Robinsons through whom she inherited further land and property in Levisham in 1841. Robert and Jane had eight children - seven daughters, and one son, another Robert. Three daughters married into local farming families - Sarah Ann marrying Samuel Scholefield, a farmer from Pickering; Adelaide a Saltersgate farmer, Newton Estill; and Amelia, George Keath of Newton who after a period of working on the railway, took over Rectory Farm in Levisham. The eldest daughter Mary Jane married a clergyman, George Terry, of Full Sutton near York, and Louisa married Thomas Truelove, draper, from Alnwick. One unmarried daughter, Harriet, died in Scarborough in 1906 at the age of 95. The son Robert went up to St Catherine's College, Cambridge in 1849, but there is no record of his having taken a degree. He married a Pickering girl, Susan Appleby, in 1859, and is known to have been living in Levisham until the 1870's. There is a brief memo in a notebook of Robert's for Monday December 13th 1869 :" My son Robert Skelton commenced teaching the school children in the Manor House Levisham, the old School House being in ruins, having been burnt down in the day", and according to the 1871 Census the Manor House was still being used as a school room, with Robert Skelton the schoolmaster.

In 1856 Robert Skelton (the Rector) suffered some sort of financial disaster[11] which necessitated selling the Hall and all his land. He was by this time a widower, and went to live with one of his married daughters, Hannah Hansell, and her husband Robert who was a Hull shipowner, at Grove House near Levisham Station, where he stayed until his death at the age of 85 in 1877.

THE RECTOR'S SON;
OR
MEMOIRS
OF
MR.JOHN SKELTON
LATE OF LEVISHAM
————-

BY JOHN WATSON

"When such a man, familiar with the skies,
Has fill'd his urn where life's pure waters rise;
And once more mingles with us meaner things,
'Tis e'en as if an angel shook his wings:
Immortal fragrance fills the circuit wide.
Which tells us whence his treasures are supplied"

————-

LONDON
PRINTED FOR THE AUTHOR:
SOLD BY JOHN MASON, 14,CITY ROAD;
AND 66,PATERNOSTER ROW

————

1833

ADVERTISEMENT

The papers of the late Mr.Skelton having been put into my hands with a request that I would prepare from them, for publication, a short narrative of his life, and make a few extracts from his Journal, the following little tract has been compiled; with a sincere desire that its perusal may promote the great object which actuated the subject of it in that labour of love from which he now rests. By these simple annals "he, being dead, yet speaketh."

J.Watson
Canterbury, Dec.15, 1832.

THE RECTOR'S SON

It is an interesting and profitable employment to place before us the examples of holy men, and to mark well the important principles which gave birth to that religious excellence by which they were distinguished through life. By this means, under the blessing of God, we may catch the spirit of emulation, and become followers of them who through faith and patience are now inheriting the promises.

John Skelton. the subject of this memoir, was the son of Robert Skelton, Rector of Levisham, at which place he was born, August 27th 1793. From his earliest childhood he appears to have been under the influence of divine impressions. When he was but a youth, a pious female, who was an inmate in the family, gave him a book on religious subjects, which awakened his attention to the realities of eternity, and checked him in the pursuit of those vanities by which he was surrounded . But he went on sinning and repenting till the spring of 1821, when he was invited by a friend to the Wesleyan chapel. After the sermon there was a love-feast, and he obtained a note of admission. On this occasion the power of the Spirit was eminently present; and while Mr.Skelton was listening to the people of God speaking of the majesty of his kingdom, and declaring his mighty acts, he felt determined to devote himself, body, soul, and spirit, a living sacrifice, holy and acceptable unto God, convinced that it was a reasonable service. He continued to seek the Lord with strong cries and tears for a few days, and then by faith he realized such a discovery of the willingness and ability of Christ to save him as enabled him to say with confidence, "He hath loved me, and given himself for me."

Having thus experienced a sense of the divine favour, he walked in the fear of the Lord, and in the comfort of the Holy Ghost. He attended to that important injunction, "Enter into thy closet, and pray to thy Father who is in secret." He felt it necessary to "pray without ceasing," because he was unceasingly exposed to the assaults of his spiritual enemies; but praying "always with all prayer and supplication in the Spirit," he was brought off more than conqueror.

He became diligent too in searching the Scriptures, which appeared to him now an unsealed book; the "eyes of his understanding being opened," he was enabled to comprehend wondrous things out of God's law. Neither was his attention confined to the writings of the New Testament; he wished to be acquainted with the whole counsel of God, and therefore he determined to go regularly through the Bible, from Genesis to the Revelation. Tasking himself to six chapters a day with intense interest, morning, noon and evening,-

> *"He read the sacred page*
> *How Abraham was the friend of God on high;*
> *Or Moses bade eternal warfare wage*
> *With Amalek's ungracious progeny;*
> *Or how the royal bard did groaning lie*
> *Beneath the stroke of Heaven's avenging ire;*
> *Or Job's pathetic plaint and wailing cry;*
> *Or rapt Isaiah's wild seraphic fire;*
> *Or other holy seers that tuned the sacred lyre."*

The promises of the Gospel especially were to him sweeter than honey or the honey-comb; and having for some time enjoyed the blessing of justification, he was ardently desirous of possessing the fulness of the Spirit. He saw that it was his privilege to be saved from inward as well as outward sin; to have the thoughts of his heart cleansed by the inspiration of God's Holy Spirit; and thus, hungering and thirsting after righteousness, he was filled unutterably full of glory and of God. "Where sin abounded, grace did much more abound;" and having borne the image of the earthly, he now bore the image of the heavenly :"a living epistle, known and read of all men."

His relatives, of course, could not be ignorant of the great change which was wrought in him; and perceiving the new bent and bias of his mind, they wished him to become a clergyman of the established church, and advised him to enter a course of preparatory study; but his zeal for the salvation of souls impelled him to begin at once to endeavour to snatch them from "everlasting burnings." His yearning pity for mankind prevented him from remaining silent, and he says, "My plan was this: to visit the sick, and assist at prayer-meetings, and speak to all to whom I had access respecting spiritual and eternal things."

Sometimes God has made known to his people his providential designs by dreams and visions of the night. It was by dreaming of the sheaves of corn, and the sun and moon and eleven stars, that Joseph became acquainted with his future destiny; and a dream no less singular, which Mr Skelton had in the month of December, left an impression upon his mind, that, if he improved the grace which had been already given him, he would afterwards have to come forward more publicly in calling sinners to repentance. He dreamed that he was in a place resembling a room, at the end of which a man with a hammer was employed in making an aperture in the wall. To this his attention was directed, and, walking up to it, he looked through the opening into a dark cavern. On enquiring the name of the place, the man replied, "That, Sir, is hell; the place into which David says, the wicked shall be turned, with all nations that forget God." And then he stated to him, that he heard distinctly the howlings of the damned. At this he was so terrified, that he exclaimed with earnestness, "Save, Lord, or I perish;" and shortly afterwards, a friend pointed him to a small door, through which, with considerable difficulty, he escaped from his apparently perilous situation. He then awoke, thankful that ever he was made a subject of the converting grace of God, and by flying for refuge to the Lord Jesus Christ, had actually realized the deliverance from future wrath, of which this was a lively representation. He continued to give evidence of the sincerity of his profession, by deep personal piety, and an increasing concern for the prosperity of Zion, and in a few months he was proposed and accepted as a Local Preacher. He was deeply conscious of much unfitness for so important an office, but his dream was still vividly impressed upon his mind, and he dared not refuse the call of the church to serve his generation according to the will of God. He could truly say with Cecil, "Hell is before me, and thousands of souls shut up there in everlasting agonies. Jesus Christ stands forth to save men from rushing into this bottomless abyss. He sends me to proclaim his ability and love. I want no fourth idea! Every fourth idea is contemptible! Every fourth idea is a grand impertinence!" Stimulated by such convictions, he was instant in season and out of season, endeavouring to turn the hearts of the disobedient to the wisdom of the just.

Neither did he labour in vain, or spend his strength for naught. The great Head of the Church, who condescends to employ the weak things of the world to confound the things that are mighty, crowned the labours of his servant with abundant success, wherever he went publishing the good news of the kingdom. Not only in the villages of his own neighbourhood, but also in the Malton, Whitby and other Circuits which he was in the habit of visiting, he saw signs and wonders effected by the plain and pointed announcement of the doctrines of our holy Christianity. He was a man, like Barnabas, full of faith and of the Holy Ghost. He honoured God by relying implicitly upon the promises of the Gospels, and God honoured him in making him an instrument of much spiritual good. The weapons of his warfare were not carnal, but mighty through God to the pulling down of strong holds. It was no unusual thing for three or four, and sometimes a dozen, individuals, to be labouring under deep conviction of sin, and seeking the Lord with their whole heart under his ministry, and at the prayer-meetings which he held invariably after the preaching.

> *"Truth from his lips prevailed with double sway,*
> *And fools who came to scoff remained to pray."*

On one occasion, during his excursions of usefulness, he met with a Roman Catholic whose mind had been enlightened to see the errors of popery, and was enquiring for a more excellent way. He directed him to look by simple faith to the Lamb of God, who taketh away the sin of the world; and while they were earnestly praying together, the poor papist devotee was enabled to believe to the saving of his soul. In recording this circumstance in his journal, which he kept from the time of his conversion, Mr.Skelton emphatically adds, "Praise God for a Roman Catholic. God grant that such conversions may become more frequent. May the time soon arrive, when the man of sin, the son of perdition, whose coming is after the working of Satan, with all power, and signs, and lying wonders, and deceivableness of unrighteousness, shall be destroyed by the Spirit of his mouth, and consumed by the brightness of his coming,"

The secret of his usefulness was this, he insisted every where upon the necessity of seeking a present salvation. Knowing that the kingdon of heaven suffereth violence, and that it is the violent who take it by force, he laboured with all his might to persuade sinners immediately to repent, immediately to believe the Gospel; at the same time believing himself for the promised outpouring of the Holy Spirit. He strongly insisted that the knowledge of salvation by the remission of sins was not confined to the primitive Christians, but offered with equal freeness to those who heard him. Reader, hast thou this knowledge? If not, dost thou desire to have it? Seek it now, seek it by simple faith, there is no other way of obtaining it.

> *"Faith, mighty faith, the promise sees,*
> *And looks to that alone."*

What is the promise? "He that believeth shall be saved." "Though your sins be as scarlet, they shall be whiter than the snow; though they be red like crimson, they shall be as wool." Faith lays hold, with a tenacious grasp, upon this truth of God,

> *"Laughs at impossibilities,*
> *And cries, It shall be done."*

In August, Mr.Skelton was rather discouraged on account of the prayer-meetings being so thinly attended, but this led him to pray more earnestly: "For Zion's sake will I not rest, and for Jerusalem's sake will I not hold my peace, until the righteousness thereof go forth as a lamp that burneth." His soul was considerably blessed while attempting to improve the death of the Rev. George Sargent, who was killed by the upsetting of a coach on his way to the Sheffield Conference. In a few days after this he writes : "A glorious work broke out in Lockton; six souls were set at liberty, and several more were under conviction. The first I observed to be in distress was a young woman, who continued in deep anguish for several hours, but no sooner had she experienced the efficacy of the Saviour's blood, than she began to pray, with the courage of an old Christian, for the salvation of others. O Lord, carry on thy work till thy praises are echoed from shore to shore, and the "kingdoms of this world become the kingdoms of our God and of his Christ."

This extraordinary revival produced a strong sensation in the neigh-bourhood; and many adversaries, bold, voluble, and impudent, were heard contradicting and blaspheming. Many, who were warm and active enough in temporal things, pronounced those who were engaged in this good work enthusiasts; and no wonder, for they had not spiritual discernment to discover, that whether they were beside themselves it was for God, or whether they were sober, it was for their cause. But though they knew it not, "He that winneth souls is wise," no matter who accounts him a fool; and they who "turn many to righteousness shall shine as the brightness of the firmament, and as the stars for ever and ever."

Mr.Skelton had no notion of a religion without feeling; his first object was to make people feel their guilt and danger as sinners; and then he exhorted them to rest not till they felt the love of God shed abroad in their hearts by the Holy Ghost given unto them. Visiting a woman who was confined to her room through indisposition, and burdened with a sense of the sins she had committed, he told her, that God could remove the burden and make her happy. "Oh," she said, "this is what I should like." He then requested her to pray, and she cried out, "Lord, help me; Lord, have mercy upon me; for Christ's sake, remove this burden." Then a ray of hope seemed to penetrate the clouds of darkness which rolled around her; and after wrestling for some time in continued importunate prayer, the star of Jacob appeared, and she was able to testify that God for Christ's sake had indeed blotted out her transgressions. Believing with her heart unto righteousness, with her mouth she made confession unto salvation.

February 12. *- He says, "An awful judgment has arrested a swearer. While uttering a shocking imprecation, about nine o'clock this morning, a horse struck him in the forehead, and about four o'clock in the afternoon he entered eternity. Thus the wicked is driven away in his wickedness. ' O that men were wise, that they understood this, that they would consider their latter end.' "*

About the same time he records the case of a gentleman who had been drinking at an inn until late on a Sunday night, instead of remembering the day of the Lord, to keep it holy; and on returning home, he missed his way in the dark, forcing his horse over a tremendous precipice, and was dashed to pieces, a warning to all Sabbath-breakers.

April 27. *- He writes, " At a prayer-meeting, several individuals found peace with God. One of these was a young man who was quite deaf. I put a paper into his hand, giving an account of the conversion of a little girl. He read it twice over with serious attention, and after some conversation by writing upon a slate he*

became powerfully affected, knelt down and earnestly pleaded with God to save him. While we were singing
        "Ah, write the pardon on my heart," etc /
he arose from his knees and wrote upon the slate, "I cannot tell one half of what I feel." After the meeting he went home and found his father, who for two years had been seeking the Lord, praying in his closet for the salvation of his soul. He threw his arms around his father's neck, told him what he had experienced, and from that time father and son went on their way rejoicing."
        The following places are mentioned as scenes of labour in which God was pleased to display his divine power in the awakening and converting of sinners.
        "I have met," he says, " with upwards of five hundred who have professed to find peace with God, and forty-one who have experienced a deeper work of God in their hearts. These are scattered abroad in Stockton, York, Knaresborough, Whitby, Robin Hood's Bay, Glazedale, Fryup, Harrogate, Green Hammerton, etc. Well might the prophet ask, 'Who is a God like unto thee, that pardoneth iniquity, and passeth by the transgressions of the remnant of his heritage?' 'He retaineth not his anger for ever, because he delighteth in mercy.'"

> *"Mercy he doth for thousands keep;*
> *He goes and seeks the long-lost sheep,*
> *And brings his wanderer home.*
> *And every soul that sheep might be:*
> *Come then, my Lord, and gather me;*
> *My Jesus, quickly come."*

        Some of Mr.Skelton's friends were apprehensive that his great exertions in prayer and preaching would shorten his days, and they endeavoured to persuade him to desist; but the word of the Lord was like fire in his bones, and he still went on reproving and rebuking and exhorting with all long-suffering and doctrine, travailing in birth for penitent sinners till Christ was formed in them the hope of glory. There can be no doubt that his health was poured forth as a libation upon the altar of the church, for it now became evident that disease was preying powerfully upon his vitals; and yet, however he might be censured for imprudence, he seems to have thought that the sacrifice was not too costly in a cause for which the Redeemer shed his most precious blood. He literally counted not his life dear unto hmself that he might finish his course with joy, and the ministry he had received of the Lord Jesus, to testify the Gospel of the grace of God. And how is it possible for a Christian to be properly impressed with the worth of souls,. and not put forth his utmost energies to promote their salvation? The bare possibility of souls being lost, - lost for ever, - should exterminate every feeling of indifference. "For what," it has been asked, "if it be lawful to indulge such a thought, what would be the funeral obsequies of a lost soul? Would it suffice for the sun to veil his face, and the moon her brightness? to cover the heavens with sackcloth, and the ocean with mourning? Or, if all nature could become animated and vocal, would it be possible to utter a groan too deep, or a cry too piercing, to furnish an adequate idea of the magnitude and extent of such a catastrophe?"
        In the summer of 1830, his health continuing to decline, he writes, "I have been led as much as possible to look death full in the face, and I think I now feel the point of his lance in my breast. How shall I sufficiently praise the Lord for this day's experience. O what sweet composure of mind do I realize! no corroding

cares, no perplexing fears. I feel the hallowing influence of the Spirit of God; that influence which gives wings to my soul, and assures me, that if I fail on earth I shall rise to life eternal."

July 4th. *- "My old friend, the Rev.J.M-[12], called to see me this morning; but he only remained a short time, as he had to be engaged in the work of the Lord in Glazedale and Fryup. Farewell, brother , M -, success to thy labours! It may well be we shall never meet again on earth; but I look forward in confidence to meet thee in heaven. Blessed be the name of the Lord : if the next meeting be above, we will tell of the triumphs we saw on earth, and shout the praises of Jehovah for ever.*

19th. *- "This day, by the assistance of a stick, I have travelled a short distance along one of my favourite walks. The village, the place of my birth, just before me, the beauty of the surrounding scenery, the doves cooing in the woods, and the larks ascending in the air, warbling their Creator's praise, all presented subjects of contemplation to my mind. Here too my attention was sweetly occupied in thinking upon the blessed work of bringing lost sinners to God."*

Sept.21. *- "Last night, after retiring to bed, and being unable to lie upon either side for pain, my mind was borne away in meditation to a milder region. I felt as if within the very suburbs of heaven, and I thought I saw a number of my departed friends, and that I heard them say, 'Skelton is on his way, he is coming home, let us go to the bank of death to meet him.' This caused tears of joy to start into my eye, and filled my soul with holy rapture. I cried out, 'Stay, friends, till I have weathered out the storm, and with you I'll traverse the eternal plains of pleasure; with you I'll gaze upon the glorious scars of our Redeemer; and with you, in loudest strains, standing before the triune God, I'll strike my harp for ever.'"*

The following account of his last moment is from the pen of his brother, the Rev. Robert Skelton, the present Rector of Levisham, in a letter to Mr.William Bowes, of West-Bolden.

August 12th,1831. *- "It hath pleased the Head of the church to take unto himself the soul of my dear brother. This expected event took place last Lord's day, about a quarter before eight o'clock, A M. His last hour was an hour of bitter suffering; but, glory be to God, he could praise his holy name, and say, 'Thy will be done!' In the former part of the week I administered the sacrament to him, and it was indeed a profitable season to us both. The last petition that he offered was, 'Come, Lord Jesus, come quickly;' and shortly afterwards he entered into rest. May we, dear Sir, copy his bright example; and may our last end be, like his, all resignation and peace."*

Such was the man whose character is here faintly delineated; a man who lived for eternity; a man whose sole concern was the glory of God, and the advancement of his own spiritual interests and those of his species; and in comparison with whom numbers, it is to be feared, in the great day of final decision, will be found to have spent their days in laborious uselessness, "dropping buckets into empty wells, and growing old with drawing nothing up!"

His remains were interred in the aisle of Levisham Church, and many a countenance in the long and lingering procession attendant at his funeral, looked indicative of what was no doubt the sentiment of the heart, -

> *"In silent anguish, O, my friend,*
> *While I recall thy worth,*
> *Thy lovely life, thy early end,*
> *I seem estranged from earth;*
> *My soul with thine desires to rest,*
> *Supremely and for ever blest."*

A LEVISHAM FARM-WORKER'S YEAR
1913

JOHN BROUGH'S DIARY

This is the diary for the year 1913 of a young man working on a farm in Levisham. He was a dedicated diarist, making an entry for every day of the year, recording in a straightforward, factual way the day's events, starting with the time he got up and usually finishing with a note about the weather - something that was always of importance to someone working out of doors, exposed to the elements! His plain, unadorned but accurate prose style matches his subject matter, bare statements of what happened with little description, occasional comments showing a dry sense of humour.

His diaries for several years are in the possession of his son, another John Brough, who has transcribed them, deciphering writing done with sometimes poor quality pencils by candle light in the stable at the end of the day. Occasionally there are words that could not be read, and occasionally something has been added in[ ] for elucidation. Otherwise, the diary is as young John Brough wrote it in 1913.

Some people who keep diaries write for themselves alone; some have an eye to other readers. John finishes his first entry on January 1st with the greeting: " wishing all people who read this a happy New Year" as though he is one of the second group. He had the writer's urge to set down his story in words, and after a long day at the plough or in the harvest field, thought it all worth recording.

The diary gives direct insight into life in Levisham and Newtondale just before the 1st World War. It is written in colloquial language using the local

---

With **THREE** Insurance Coupons.

"GOSSAMER"

POCKET DIARY,

1913.

———

ONE DAY ON A PAGE.

Series No. 44.

	NET.
Leatherette Cover, Flush, Plain	-/6
Leather Flush, Marbled	1/-
Leather Back Loop Case	1/3
French Morocco Tuck Case, Two Pockets ..	1/6
Superior Leather Case, with Pockets	2/6

———

London:

STRAKER & CRANE'S DIARY CO., LTD.,

PUBLISHING DEPOT —

38, KING WILLIAM STREET, E.C.

Sold by all Stationers and Booksellers.

idiom which sometimes needs interpreting for "foreigners" who do not know that "roak" is mist, or that "slape" is "slippery" (both, incidentally, words of Norse origin, relics of a Viking past). After a spell of bad weather, it "fairs up"; when anyone has been away, they "land" home again. The meaning is usually clear even when the words are unfamiliar and not found in a dictionary, but a glossary has been added to explain some of the unusual words. He writes about "our folks" : his parents, Absalom and Mary Brough, his older brother Tom who lived at home and ran the farm, his sisters Hannah (at home),Polly (sometimes spelled Pollie),married to Manny(sometimes Mannie) Baldwin,who were in the process of moving to Saintoft Cottage but were at Wet Head for the first months of the year, and Jenny who lived further up Newtondale at Bumble Bee Hall. When he is up at Levisham, "our folks" become the Keaths where he was working. He writes about Newtondale neighbours: Milestones, Pashbys, Pickerings; about the people who were part of his working life and those with whom he shared his leisure; about Sundays at home relaxing after the strenuous work of the week, which is what occupied most of his time and so appropriately occupies most of his diary. One day's entry finishes " *I think there is nothing very important today.*" This could be the text for the whole diary ; it is the essence of the everyday life of most people, and the monotony that comes through in reading the diary is perhaps a salutary corrective to any nostalgic longings for the simplicity of the old days, or romanticism about country life. A problem about any diary of daily life is that it is of necessity repetititive. John Brough's equivalent to Pepys' " ...and so to bed" is " Got up at five...", the prelude to a day of strenuous phyisical work for what seem to us in our affluent age to be remarkably few material rewards - yet at the end he is able to say : "*..taking it altogether, it has been a very good year as far as I am concerned*".

Wet Head

At the beginning of the year, John was at home at Wet Head,in the parish of Newton-on-Rawcliffe, one of the small, isolated farms that are dotted round the Newtondale area. Immediately below the farm, the land falls away in a steep escarpment down into Newtondale with at the bottom the railway built by George Stephenson in 1836 to link Whitby with Pickering; Levisham station is about a quarter of a mile down the line. To the south is a smaller valley in which Raindale Beck flows down into Newtondale. Beyond Raindale, an area of open moorland, Stony Moor,then after another deep valley, the village of Newton, with a population in 1913 of around 200. Nearer to Wethead than Newton is Stape, an outlying area of Pickering parish. It has no real village centre, but consists of scattered farms. In John Brough's time Stape had two active Methodist chapels, a school, and the Stape band which continues to this day. From Wethead, you look across the narrow defile of Newtondale to Levisham moor with Levisham village out of sight beyond it, near as the crow flies but reached by a stiff climb. These places provide the setting for John Brough's narrative.

The Brough family had been in the Newtondale area for at least two generations. John's grandfather Thomas Brough is listed in the 1841 and 1851 censuses in the Raindale area, and in 1861 was farming 30 acres at King Richard's House, Stape. John's father Absalom was at one time a blacksmith; by the time of the 1881 census he was at Wet Head farming 36 acres, married to

Wet Head.

Mary Jane Winspear and with a growing family of whom John, born 1894, was the youngest.The farm was rented from the Keldy Castle Estate, and is shown at the time of the sale of the estate in 1893 as paying an annual rental of £16. It was a small operation, run mainly by John's older brother Tom and not doing well enough in 1913 to carry a second son on its pay-roll. Absalom was then 76, and the small mention of him in the diary suggests he no longer took an active part in the running of the farm. Tom and John spent most of their time working outside, looking after the livestock - mainly cows, but also sheep and a pig,- growing potatoes, turnips, hay. There was maintenance work to be done on the roads around the farm, trees to be felled and firewood chopped.Like many of the small farmers of the Newtondale area they supplemented their income by making besoms[13] out of ling from the moors bound with lappings of ash bark, which were taken down to Pickering for sale to agents who supplied them in large quantities to northern foundries where they were used for skimming impuities from the molten metal.

The women of the family did the indoor work,- baking, churning, washing, mending are all referred to. Mrs Brough was in poor health during the year and not able to get about or do much; in October there is a reference to her being *"a nice lot better"* and able to get about with a stick and milk regularly, and by November she was able to do *"a tremendous lot of work now"*, feeding and milking the cows, though still with a swollen and painful leg. The housekeeping seems to have been a bit haphazard, with occasions when they *"run short of eatables"*, have to make a few cakes over the fire or have to dispatch Tom to Newton for flour *"first thing, as we had nothing to eat"*. Hannah lived at home with her 6 year old daughter Frances, going out to work irregularly at one or two places including the Keaths at Levisham. Polly and her husband Manny had "flitted" from Marton to Saintoft Cottage, a few miles away in the direction of Pickering, on January 4th, but did not actually move in there till later in the year, waiting perhaps until after their new baby was born. This event is noted between the fetching of a load of straw and the sermon preached by Mr Temple (*"no converts this time"*) on Monday, February 10th - *"Polly got a baby boy tonight, born a bit after nine, so we had a bit of a bustle on."* There was no calling out of a doctor or midwife; just the help of a neighbour, Mrs Milestone.

Chapel Culture

A century after John Skelton's time, the bubbling evangelical fervour of the original Methodist revival had been institutionalised. Every village had its Wesleyan and/or Primitive Methodist chapel, ministered to mainly by Local Preachers.

The Broughs, along with their neighbours the Milestones and Pickerings, were part of the widespread Methodist community in the Newtondale area. Wet Head was on the rota for house meetings on Sunday afternoons,when the room had to be *"sided up"* and there could be *"a great fuss on"* to get everything ready. After the meeting, the preacher was likely to be entertained to tea. Later some of the family were usually up at Stape chapel for Sunday evening service.The diary notes other chapel events during the year. On Good Friday there was an entertainment in Stape chapel - not necessarily something of a sacred nature; the local paper reports Good Friday concerts in various Methodist chapels of the area with very unsacred-sounding titles- followed by a supper. In the summer there was a round of anniversaries at Wesleyan and Primitive Methodist chapels of the surrounding villages when it was necessary to be there in good time to get a seat. There were Camp Meetings, big open air gatherings with a popular appeal that had always been part of the Primitive Methodist culture -in Stape on June 22nd, Newton July 13th, the Dale July 20th where there was a *"nice gathering"* in the afternoon and as many at night when there was a Love Feast. From time to time there was a mission led by one of the local preachers - Mr Temple conducted one in Stape in February, Miss Harland a two week mission in Lockton in October and in Newton in November.

Chapel-going was a regular part of John's life, the place to go on a Sunday evening expecting to meet friends, sometimes to disturb the preacher by being noisy (May 4th),perhaps to hear something interesting - *"he talked very well"* (Sept. 14th), or not - *"didn't reckon much to his talk"*; perhaps to see *"a certain young lady..."*. Its function was social as much as religious.

Looking for Work

During January, while still working on the farm, John was trying to get a job with the railway. He filled in forms, collected references, applying for a job as a railway porter, but was disappointed to discover that the minimum age was 20. He wrote off again saying he was interested in any job that was going, and was again disappointed. The opportunity then came to work for William Keath who farmed at Levisham . It seems as if the Broughs knew the Keaths quite well. George Keath,William and Jane's father, came from Newton. At the time when his children were growing up he had been working on the railway and living in one of the railway cottages in Newtondale, where Keaths and Broughs would have been near neighbours. Later he moved to Rectory Farm in

Keath's farm is the house with the gabled roof. The building to its right was the Band Room.

Levisham where William and Jane stayed after their parents' death. Both Tom and Hannah went there to lend a hand from time to time. In February, John started working for William Keath regularly, spending Monday to Saturday in Levisham, going home from Saturday night till Monday morning.

Keath's Farm, Levisham

William and Jane Keath were the unmarried son and daughter of George Keath and Amelia, daughter of Robert Skelton, Rector of Levisham from 1818 - 1877. On George Keath's death in 1911 William took over the 100 acre farm (the third largest of the 8 farms in Levisham village), rented from the Rev. W.J.E.Armstrong, rector of Levisham[14]. In 1913, Jane was 54, William 43. They were farming on a considerably bigger scale than at Wet Head, but the impression is of hard work for small rewards : no indications of comfort around the house, or money to spare.

Jane comes across as something of a martinet and a parsimonious housekeeper. *"We only had a half meat pie warmed up for our dinner, and not very fresh at that"*, (Feb.14th)"; *"the boy and I were by ourselves, so we did full justice to our scanty fare"*, (June 20th); *"we had some fried meat at dinner-time which was set fit for a dog it was so old"* (Aug.23rd). If Jane was up late, there was no breakfast (Aug.11th). William visited relations in Hartlepool and came back on November 19th with *"a great parcel of kippers"* : *"it will be kipper supper now for a fortnight!"*. The local lads recognised Jane as someone to be provoked: *"the mill boy came up and was shouting among the other boys against our gate and annoyed Jane with his bad language"* (June 26th); when sheltering in the quarry with Willie Hart, *"he said some fond things about Miss Keath"* (Nov.17th); *"Miss Keath was peeping about when I came in at dinner* time..."(Nov 4th); *"Miss Keath was rather vexed..."*(Nov 1st); *"old Jane was in a rage.."* (May 9th).. There was a lightening of the atmosphere on occasions when Jane was not there; *"we had a good laugh at dinner-time, as William went to the station with Jane in the trap and we had our dinners alone"*(May 19th), and on another occasion when the two boys were having their supper on their own they had *"such a laughing going on as never was....."* (Aug. 25th).There are few comments about William Keath. He is there sharing in the daily work of the farm, but no impression comes across of what he was like as a person.

When John first went to work at Levisham, there was "old Ned " working at Keath's. He disappears from the scene fairly soon after being unwell- *"bad with a cold"*, *"bad with indigestion"* and a boy was taken on who is generally referred to simply as "the boy", but is sometimes named as Harold. When "we" take out the horses, or work together, or go to the reading room in the evening, one assumes it is John and Harold. In November, Harold was thinking about his future : *"Harold has seen some soldiers at Pickering and he is considering whether to join the army or stay in farming"* (Nov.17th).In 1913, "joining the army" would have conjured up pictures of a life of discipline with adventure, not the as yet unimagined horrors of the Flanders killing-fields, while farming offered the all too well known routines with no exciting prospects for a young man.

Leisure

The diary makes clear how little leisure there was in a farm worker's life. Working from before six in the morning till night for six days a week did not leave much time for oneself, but there were Sundays and there were the evenings.

John's diary-writing is evidence of his literary bent, so it is not surprising to find that he liked reading - *"had a peaceful read over the fire"*, (Jan 8th); *"stayed at home and read the papers"*, (May 2nd); *"was reading till late"*, (May 17th). What was there to read? The papers are mentioned several times, and on July 6th *"I have been having a right good read today, been reading the stories in the Sunday Circle and in the Companion"*. These papers had more of a literary function than today's newspapers, incorporating short stories and serials for readers who had no other easy access to fiction.

Music played a big part in his leisure time. He and Tom were members of the Stape band, as was William Keath, John playing both cornet and melodeon. The diary opens in the new year when the band was on its round of the neighbourhood, playing at Pickering, at various villages - Cropton, Wrelton, Hartoft, and around less populated areas like Raindale, Stony Moor, Flamboro' Rigg. There was a lot of pleasure and a useful bit of pocket money from it. Going up to the bandroom at Stape to practice was a regular Sunday occupation, and there were unofficial bits of practice some evenings. There was an old house in Raindale used as a bandroom, and old photographs of Levisham show a bandroom attached to the side of one of the farm houses. It.was a matter to record when Tom lost the mouthpiece of John's cornet, and relief when it was found again. On Whit Monday, May 12th, the Band had an engagement to play *"at the picnic on the island at Egton Bridge."* They started at 2pm playing for dancing all afternoon and evening, then walked home, arriving at 1am *"plugging tired"* - late up next morning! John's accounts, which record every

Stape Band, a few years before John Brough joined it.

Back Row: James Brough (John's brother), Thomas Peirson, Thomas Holliday, Thomas Fletcher, William Watson; *Middle Row:* Edward Greenheld, John Eddon (Snr), John WM Baker, John Hugill; *Front Row:* John Eddon (Jnr), Ernest Woodmansey, William Denniel Joseph Fletcher, William Peirson, John Nicholes.

item of income and expenditure, however small, show 3 shillings received "*for playing at Egton Bridge";* a welcome addition to a week's wage of 9 shillings.Sometimes there was singing - there is reference to a "*singing practice at the Baker's*" and a few days later "*went to Mr Baker's at night to have a sing, and we stayed there till after ten".(*Jan 27th).

In December, John bought a second-hand gramophone from his friend Arthur Magson for 6 shillings. This went up to Levisham where he entertained himself with it in the barn at night. His appetite for gramophones had been whetted, and he wrote off for catalogues, intending to get a better model.

Social life in Levisham went on in the evenings in the Reading Room, (now the Village Hall), which had been provided for the village at the expense of the Rector, the Rev. W.J.E.Armstrong. Here there was a fire - two when it was really cold, a place to play bagatelle and to read the paper. There was the predictable difference in tastes between the young who were seen by their elders as too noisy and the older set who wanted a quiet place to sit and natter : "*was down at the reading room at night, but they were sat in the dark, and we made too much noise for them*" (Apr.25th);"*was down at the reading room at night and there is awful dozy doing down there*" (March 20th). In the summer there were the more active recreations of cricket and quoits: quoits had the advantage of not needing so many players. The boys in the village had a harder working life than youngsters today, but here they sound very much the same : "*I went down in the coke hole under the church with Jack, Tom and party and, my word, we did enjoy ourselves, I was laughing all the time*". Apart from his sisters, girls are hardly mentioned: just one coy reference to "*a certain young lady whom I had come on purpose to see* "(Nov.30th).

In the summer there was more going on. John biked into Pickering with a friend on July 30th to the Circus, which he judged "pretty fair". Newton tea feast (July 2) he found "rather tame"; Levisham show on August 2nd was more fun, with sports and competitions in the evening as well as prizes for stock and garden produce. Ryedale show finished with fireworks (August 12th) while Whitby regatta was a big enough event for John to have a day off work to go with his friends by train to join the crowds .It was "*a beautiful day*", with plenty to enjoy even though the crowds obscured the races and made it hard to keep with his friends. John spent more money that day on enjoyment than any other time in the year - 2s3d on the train fare, and various small purchases including a tin whistle and a mouth organ, which he had fun teaching himself to play over the next few weeks.

Fireworks on November 5th were a rather paltry affair, "*dozey*" in John's terminology, which some of the village boys had been collecting for a few weeks earlier. The "tar barrel" referred to (Oct.17th) was a local custom when children dressed up and went round singing the traditional song and begging for money.

The Hiring Fair in November brought crowded streets in Pickering, barrel organs playing popular tunes, and sideshows. Harold left, his term of employment ended. John's was a more flexible arrangement with William Keath so he did not take the usual Martinmas Week holiday as he could take a day off when he needed one.

Communications

The coming of the railway between Whitby and Pickering in 1836 must have been an event of revolutionary significance to the people living in the area. Not only was the train there for local passenger and goods traffic, but the remote area of Newtondale was opened up to people from further afield. Rural life had attractions for those penned up in the big cities, and wealth made in industry could be used to buy a country property for purposes of sport or retirement. Barnes Wimbush who bought Levisham Hall in 1891 came from London, interested in the shooting and fishing .John Tomlinson who came to The Rowl a few years later was a rubber manufacturer from Leeds.

Since the coming of the railway, there had been no major new developments in communication. Cars were not yet in general use - there is one reference in the diary to a car, Tom Snowden's motor car (July 6th). To get to Pickering, there was the train or bicycle or horse, or you could walk, - and to people who have come to look on walking of any distance as a leisure activity, done on special occasions and needing the right gear, it comes as a surprise to see the distances that John walked in the ordinary course of daily life. First thing every Monday morning he walked to Levisham, back again to Wet Head after work on Saturday night; he walked from Wet Head to Stape, to Newton, to Saintoft, all in the course of a working life spent almost entirely on his feet, walking. Today the railway that still runs up Newtondale operates as a tourist attraction, staffed partly by volunteers enjoying an exercise in nostalgia, while the serious business of transporting goods and people round the area is done by lorry and car on the roads. It is hard for us to appreciate what it meant to people a century ago who depended on it to to get them to Pickering market, on an outing to Whitby regatta, to get about on business or for pleasure.

Something we might find particularly disconcerting is the absence of the telephone, which in 1913 was still a rarity. When the vet was needed urgently for a mare in trouble, John had to borrow a bike and pedal the six miles to Pickering. Would the mare have been saved if it had been possible to get to the vet sooner ? When he wanted to get a message home, John would go down to the station in the hope that one of "our folks" would be passing. There was no way of sending a message to Levisham when he was not well enough to get to work one Monday morning, nor for Tom to let the family know he was not getting home one night The railway had a system of conveying by basket - *"Mannie went to the station to get the basket"*, (Jan.17th), *"Tom had to go to the station with the basket,"* (Jan 31st), *"I took the basket to the station"*,(Feb 7th).

Villages were of necessity much more self-contained units than we are used to today. Sometimes William or Jane would go down to Pickering on a Monday - Market Day; sometimes John went to Pickering after work on a Saturday and shopped there for some of his clothes. But Lockton could supply a tailor, a general shop, a blacksmith, and hair-cutting could be done by a neighbour. John cycled into Pickering after work one Saturday evening, and the shops were still open for him to buy a pair of boots at 8pm. For people working long hours every day of the week, Saturday evening was the only opportunity for shopping.

John thought nothing of walking or cycling the hilly routes between Levisham, Newton, Stape and Saintoft week after week, but seldom travelled further afield. During the year, his trip by train to Whitby for the regatta (about 20 miles to the north) and a cycle ride to Malton (about 12 miles to the south) are the furthest places he visited. Compared with their successors today, the inhabitants of Levisham in 1913 must have known intimately the roads and lanes, the fields and hedgerows of their immediate neighbourhood but only sketchily anywhere beyond. Their society was geographically confined to the villages and towns within reach by horse-drawn vehicles, bicycle, on foot, or which were on or near the railway line.

Farm Work

Most of the diary is concerned with work, first at Wet Head, then at Keath's farm at Levisham. From this day-by-day account we can build up a picture of the working of a small moorland-village farm.

An imaginary Job Specification for a farm worker in John's position might have looked something like this :

Young man with plenty of stamina needed, not afraid of hard work.

Pay: 9 shillings per week, plus board and lodging. Bonus at harvest time.

Hours : 5.30am(approx) to dusk, Monday - Saturday; meal breaks breakfast and dinner. Earlier finish Saturday evenings. Overtime at harvest.

Holiday : Martinmas week

Skills needed: must be able to care for and work with horses, and share in all aspects of farm work.

Work mainly with horses, PLOUGHING, drilling, scruffling, harrowing, haymaking, raking, reaping; hoeing by hand; mowing with scythe; stack-making and thatching; sheep shearing; milking; general maintenance work in farm yard, out buildings, and fields; carting loads by wagon on the farm, also to and from the station. Willingness to give help on other farms expected on occasions.

Horse power

This was farming before the days of tractors, when the pulling-power on the farm came from horses. As late as 1941 there was only one tractor in Levisham, and 29 horses[15]. John was working with horses most of his time. A typical day's diary entries begins *"Got up about half past five, fed the horses and cleaned them out."* In the summer, the horses stayed out in the fields and had to be fetched in the morning and taken back at night: more walking, and an earlier than usual start. Sometimes the horses are named - Bonnie,Diamond, Jet, lame Jet,- sometimes just refered to as "the mare", so it is hard to be sure how many horses were kept. Two foals were born during the year; one died (April 1st), and one mare died in March. Usually the horses worked in pairs, yoked to the plough or harrow or digger or reaper; sometimes a team of three was needed as when, for example, a heavy load of coal had to be fetched up from the station in the wagon. There were few days in the year when the horses were not working - occasionally because of bad weather, occasionally because of the nature of the work, as when all hands were needed to hoe turnips in July.

The farm grew cereal crops : wheat, oats, barley; root crops : turnips, swedes, potatoes; also rape, and "seeds", - grass, for hay. They kept cows,which were mainly the boy's responsibility so are not mentioned much until after the boy left in November when milking came into John's daily schedule. There were sheep, pigs, and the poultry which was Jane's department, as was the dairy side of things. John's sister Hannah sometimes came up to help with churning and baking. As John was working chiefly with the horses, it is the work in the fields which is recorded in most detail.

The farm had its own basic equipment, plough, roller, chain harrows, chisel harrow, scruffler, to which William added a grass reaper during the year (May

Steam engine arrives in Levisham for threshing.

29th). He had an oil engine used for chopping up animal fodder. Other equipment was borrowed or shared, The steam engine used for thrashing went the rounds of the farms during September, and there are references to borrowing a drill and a roller.At harvest time the farmers helped each other, all working till dark when the weather was fit in order to get the harvest in in time.

Calendar of Farm Work recorded by Brough, Feb. - Dec.

February
ploughing
thrashing (steam engine)

March
ploughing
thrashing
harrowing
winnowing oats
collecting thorns
drilling corn

April
lambing
harrowing, rolling, drilling
mare foaled

May
ploughing, harrowing, drilling
planting potatoes

June
sheep shearing
ploughing
stooking corn
scruffling
hoeing turnips

July
sheep dipping
ploughing, rolling, harrowing
scruffling
hay-turning (horse rake)
cocking and carting

August
scruffling
cutting and carting bracken
thatching haycocks
mowing thistles
harvesting

September
cutting oats
cutting corn, binding, stacking
raking
thrashing
mending hedges
potato picking
thatching stacks

October
sheep dipping
carting manure
ploughing
sowing wheat

November
carting slag for road
pulping and chopping turnips

December
ploughing
pulling turnips
pulping animal food
thrashing
setting nets (for sheep pens)

Ploughing was his most regular task, and there are regular entries about "setting a rig", "getting a piece rigged up", about "throwing-out pieces" and "gays". These were all technical terms in the ridge and furrow, or rig(g) and fur(r) method of ploughing, which was designed to take account of two facts : first, that a pair of horses need a wide turning circle and so cannot economically plough across a field going up and down, each furrow beside the last one; secondly, with a fixed ploughshare, furrows are always turned to the right so that if the field were ploughed in a straight up-and-down way, the furrows would form ridges and the field would have a corrugated rather than an even surface.

The ploughman started by putting a stick as a marker, then ploughed straight across to the stick, turned, ploughed back, the furrows turning inwards towards each other creating a ridge : "setting a rigg". He then ploughed in a circular pattern round the rigg he had set, all the furrows turning inwards.In a large field, there would be several riggs. The "throwing-out pieces" were ploughed differently, ploughing anti-clockwise round and round from the outside. If the field were an irregualr shape, there would be odd-shaped pieces left that did not fit into the riggs or the throwing-out pieces: these were the "gays". Finally, the headlands round the edge of the field would be ploughed. This was not only a highly skilled job but one involving miles of walking[16].

Leading is a word cropping up frequently in the diary, meaning "carting". This might involve a large wagon with up to four horses to pull it, or a smaller cart with one or two horses. There was manure from the stack yard and "manishment" (fertiliser) to be transported to the fields, crops to be brought in, bracken to be cut and collected from the moor (to use as bedding for the animals, and for the stack bottoms), stakes cut from the woods to be carried for fencing, loads of grain to be taken down to the station. Off the farm, loads of chippings were brought up from the station to put down on the village lanes - a four-horse job (March7),and there was a truck of slag to be brought up from the station and taken to various points for repairing the roads. Anyone familiar with the steep hills in and out of Levisham will realise the importance of keeping them soundly surfaced. From time to time someone in the village had a truck-load of coal delivered to the station which had to be shovelled into a cart and carried load by load up the hill. Armstrong, the Rector, had several loads of coal during the year, a truckful in April, another 8 tons 16cwt in September, a load of coke in October. There was a truck load of 5tons 15cwt of coal for the Tomlinsons in June, another 5 ton load for the Keaths a few weeks later, a smaller load of four and a half tons for the Rickinsons and the schoolmistress in October, a truck for Arthur Hammond in November. When word came that a truck of coal was at the station, other work had to stop till it had been dealt with. Two days in October were spent fetching six wagon loads of stone from Newton Quarry for Ben Simpson to build a summer-house for the Armstrongs. The following month there was a truck of slag to be lead from the station for road repairs - 9tons 2cwt brought up in ten loads. When the Tomlinsons went away, their luggage was fetched and carried between home and station.

All this was heavy work often involving problems in getting the horses to pull the loads on the steep hills and on difficult terrain - *"had a bit of bother with Jet.....she would have her own way and nearly sent the wagon over the side"*,(June 25); *"we nearly had the wagon over one time when the hind wheel*

Bentham Simpson, coachman to the Rector the Rev. J. E. Armstrong, driving Bow and Dandy, outside the Primitive Methodist Chapel. (see June 5th)

went into a hole and she was standing on three, but we got her pulled out all right", (Aug.27). The treatment given to the horses sounds a bit brutal sometimes - *"William gave her a proper good thrashing....William was giving them it with a thick stick"* (July 29).

Today, any horses seen in the village are there for purposes of pleasure, not work. Tractors ply up and down the lanes, backwards and forwards across the fields, doing in a fraction of the time all the pulling that the horses used to do. Tankers deliver oil or gas for heating, lorries and delivery vans fetch and carry,- visual reminders of a changed way of life.

Scruffling was weeding between the rows of turnips with a horse-drawn scruffler. More careful weeding had to be done with a hand hoe.

Setting nets involved putting up or moving portable wire netting to form sheep fences, for example to allow the sheep into one part of a field of turnips.

Domestic life

John's was an outdoor life, so there is more in his diary about farming than housekeeping, either at Wet Head or Levisham. The little there is does not give an impression of much comfort. He and the boy, Harold, lived in at Rectory Farm, but his spare time in the evenings was usually spent either at the Reading Room or in the stable, not in the house. It was in the stable that he kept his writing materials :" *I want a little box to put my writing paper and such like things in, as they get very dirty throwing about in the stable,*" (Dec.12th), did his writing :"*I have been busy in the stable writing up my diary....*" (Oct. 21st) ,sat talking with a friend (Oct.31st), listened to the gramophone (Dec.8th), though he *"had her on in the house as well"*. On the whole, the house seems to have been the place for John to eat and sleep . It was the workplace for Jane Keath, helped by Hannah Brough who came up from time to time to assist with the churning, butter-making, baking - the same kitchen and dairy tasks that the women at Wet Head performed. At Rectory Farm, from the reference to eating supper *"in the room tonight, as they were using the kitchen table for butter making"*, (June 19th), one gathers they usually ate in the kitchen. The household was up early - between five and six in the summer, an hour or so later in winter, with the fire to be lit indoors, milking, horse-grooming outdoors, before breakfast. Everyone met again for dinner at mid-day and supper at night, then to bed by candle-light.

At Wet Head there were a lot of family comings and goings, with some of "our folks" dropping in at the weekend or being visited, with maybe an overnight stay. There was less social life at the Keath's. Once William went to visit relations at Hartlepool; a return visit was arranged but did not come off - *"Miss Keath was rather vexed"*, (Nov.1st). William and Jane do not sound particularly sociable people.

Counting the pennies

At the end of the diary are John Brough's accounts for the year, meticulously kept, with every halfpenny accounted for. *"I have been reckoning up what I have spent up to now .... and I found a few mistakes, but I have put them right and have got it to come to just as much as I have left..."*(June 4th) - the test of successful accounting! It was very much pennies that had to be counted. With an income that rarely reached £2 a month, there was not much spare cash for spending. At the Keath's, John's wages were usually nine shillings a week with extra for the long hours worked at harvest time, plus his board and lodging. From his wages, four pence went out immediately for insurance. His biggest expenditure was on clothes - about £7 out of his total annual earnings of nearly £17. He set himself up with working clothes, with a new suit, 2 new pairs of shoes, 2 hats, a top coat, as well as sundries like socks, ties, gloves. He had a sweet tooth, spending a few pence each week on sweets, a penny here, twopence there, once four pence on a half-pound of toffee. Perhaps all the sweets have some connection with the bad toothache he was suffering in the summer, culminating in a visit to the dentist in September to have teeth out at a cost of three shillings. Our consumer society is a world away from the sparseness of life for an ordinary wage-earner in 1913.

Postscript

The focus of the diary is family, farm, village, neighbourhood, not politics or international events. The storm-clouds rolling up on the international scene are hinted at only in the reference in November to Harold thinking of joining the army. The following year saw the outbreak of the 1st World War. John joined the Royal Marines. He fought at Gallipoli and then on the Western Front where in October 1917 at Passchendale Ridge he was taken prisoner and transported to Germany. He had to work down a coal mine. He still kept a diary and this record of his PoW experiences is now in the Imperial War Museum.

When he was repatriated from Fredericksfield after the Armistice, John Brough did not return to Newtondale : there was nothing for him to return to. Manny and Polly Baldwin and their young children had left Saintoft for Leeds and the higher pay of a munitions factory. In March 1917 his father Absolem died aged 79, and the family broke up. His mother, Mary Jane, joined her daughter Jenny at Bumble Bee Hall, Lythe, where she died a few months later aged 67. Tom went to Loftus where he and his wife opened a fish and chip shop. Hannah never married; she joined Polly and Manny in Leeds. but her daughter Frances could not settle there and went to join her aunt Jenny, now at Starling Castle, a small moorland farm near Hinderwell. Here she was taken ill in December 1922, and died in Whitby hospital aged only 15. She was buried at Ugthorpe. John was there, and in his inevitable diary noted,"....she looks very sweet and content, poor child. I feel so sorry for her mother having such trouble to bring her up....All went very well and we had the satisfaction of seeing her put away respectfully, and that is a lot."

JOHN BROUGH'S DIARY
1913

January 1st Wednesday
Well, it is New Year's Day once more. Tom was given this diary, but I shall use it until I get one of the other sort. I intended going with the band today, but it was late when I got done up, and Tom had gone. Besides, it looked like rain, so I stayed at home. They are going to meet at John Hugill's and play Cropton and Wrelton, then come up from Pickering with the 5 o'clock train, and supper at Nicholes's tonight. Hannah has been at Levisham. Wm Keath has been with the Stape band. Wishing all people who read this a happy New Year.

January 2nd Thursday
I did not get up very soon, so got a bad start. I milked and separated and fed the calves, then went for some potatoes for dinner. After dinner, I went with the horse to Newton for some meal, and it was dark by I got back. Saw Pollie Milestone, she was at Milestone's for the day. The band has not been out today, but went to play at Rottengill at six tonight, and went to Watson's for supper. Our Tom went, but I thought it was not worth bothering to go up there only for two houses and a supper. Fine day, Tom has been scaling mole-hills.

January 3rd Friday
Got up about 8am and foddered and helped a bit, then set off and we met at Kit Nicholes's. Played Flambro' Rigg and Keldy, then G. Southern[?] and back by Cropton Banks, Elleron and Atkinson's. We threw up for playing Stony Moor or going straight to Pierson's for supper, and it fell to go for supper. They had the gramophone of Maud Pickering going from eleven till three. Our Tom was "touched" with toothache. We hadn't any larks at Pierson's, we were too taken up with the gramophone. We borrowed a lamp to see us home. The day has been misty, but not raining.

January 4th Saturday
We did not get to bed till 4 o'clock, so took some rousing. I got to Stape by half past ten, as it was our meeting place, then we went round Hartoft. It was awfully dirty and wet walking. There were seven of us, Willie Pierson was with us for the first time. We had our tea at Hartoft, and got set off home about eight. Landed home about ten. I think we made about thirteen shillings. I cut some chop when I got back. Tom and Mannie went to flit Mannie's things from Marton to

Saintoft Cottage. They took our horse and Tom Allanson's rully and a horse from Saintoft. It came on wet during the afternoon, but faired up for us coming home.

January 5th Sunday.
I did not get up till nearly dinnertime, as I was a bit sleepy. Our folks did not land back till after dinner. It was late when they had got to Saintoft, so they stayed all night. I had to take a message to William Keath to tell him to come and help Stape band to play at Pickering tomorrow. I went over after church, I did not stay long. Tom went over to Stape at night. It has been a dull day, came on wet around five, but faired up at seven. Mannie borrowed James Pashby's paper to read the account of his brother's wedding.

January 6th Monday.
Up about eight, cleaned out the cows and foddered them. I had no time to milk, so got ready and went with the band to Pickering. Arthur Nicholes and John Hugill were the "beggars" so I had to play seconds myself. We got our dinner at Pollie Milestone's. The weather was very cold, but it did not rain. We went by the 10am train and back by the 8pm one. We went to play Middleton, and had to look a bit sharp. There were ten of us playing. We made a little over four pounds, so we did not fare so bad.

January 7th Tuesday
I did not get up till almost dinnertime as I was tired and had a bad cold. I helped to scrape the highroad, as we call it, then Tom and I ground the cutter knives, and they were awful blunt, it would take us an hour to do them. I put them on and cut some chop. Tom and I went for a stick to Raindale on our backs. We went to play on Stony Moor and at Gibson's of Raindale, then we went to the bandroom and shared up. I got 25 shillings. Altogether we got over 16 pounds. It is the finish up. Fine day, but a bit cold.

January 8th Wednesday
I did not get up very soon, as I had a very bad cold and a nasty headache. Also, Pollie and Hannah wanted to go to Saintoft Cottage to put things straight, and they started to get ready when they got up and didn't get off till twelve. Frances stayed with us. I had all to do at morning, and afternoon as well, for Tom set them to Saintoft and did not get back till dark. We got all done up by 8 o'clock, and had a peaceful read over the fire. We were to bed in good time. A fine day, but dull, I started a dess of hay and got most of it in, and cut a good heap of chop.

January 9th Thursday
Up about half past seven and, while Tom made the fire, I foddered, then we milked and I separated and fed all up. Father and Tom have been making a new sledge. I made a board and fixed it on the separator so that we shall not need a chair to put the pail on for the skim milk. We thought, as our folks had not arrived by dark, they were staying the night [at Saintoft] but Mannie walked in as we were having our tea, expecting that they would have come.He and Tom set off to look for them by Newton and then came by Hugill's [where they found them]. Our people left their things at Hugill's. Been a fine day.

January 10th Friday
I did not get up very soon, as I was tired. I foddered and milked the cows, then separated, then fed the calves and the pig. I set off for John Hugill's, Rawcliffe

Top, for the basket our folks left yesterday. When I arrived back, I got my dinner. Tom went to Newton. He went to Job's [Job Boyes, farmer & carrier] and saved five pence in the meal line from what Lumbard's charge. I went for a few old sticks up the field to burn, and also got a bit of hay in, then cut some chop, fed all up and milked. There isn't going to be a band practice till next Friday. Very raw and cold.

January 11th Saturday

Up rather late. Foddered and milked the cows, fed the calves and pig. Went and fastened the haystack down as it was awfully windy. Then I went to Tom, who was chopping down some birch trees in the whinny bank. We set a fire in some whins and had a most awful big fire. It started snowing post dinner, so I had to pull a few sheaves out of the stack, as it was too windy to get hay in. Tom and Manny snigged the sticks up that Tom cut this morning, and we only have green sticks to burn, but we have had a good fire tonight. It is snowing awful and blowing too.

January 12th Sunday

I did not get up till after nine, then had breakfast before I went out. I milked and fed all up, then I came in and had a tune on the cornet. After dinner, I watered the cows. At night, I did not go to Stape as there was too much snow on the ground. it has been snowing small stuff all day, but it is much warmer than yesterday. I should think that there is almost two foot thickness of snow on the ground now. Tom and Mannie went to Saintoft for Mannie's insurance book. We have brought the sheep into the shop[?] or they would be buried in the snow. Been snowing all day, much warmer.

January 13th Monday

I did not get up very soon and had breakfast before I went out. I foddered and milked, and fed the calves, then I did a few odd jobs till dinner. Afterwards, I got some hay and sheaves in. There was too much snow for Manny to get to Keldy, so he and Tom have been rabbiting all day. They got four couple - not bad for bits of boys- but would have got more had I been with them. Hannah went to Pickering on the 1pm train and back on the 8pm. She has been to see Mrs Brewer. It is freezing tonight. I think that Hannah has brought my melodeon from Skaife's.

January 14th Tuesday

Got up about eight, foddered the cows, then had breakfast. Afterwards, milked and fed all up. Mannie did not go to Keldy first thing, but went about nine to see if anyone was working, but no one was there. He came back, and he and Tom have been rabbiting again today, they got nine. Tom went at night to Pickering with seven couple. Hannah has been working at Levisham. Mannie and I got a dess of hay in the afternoon. It has begun to thaw a bit tonight, I believe, but only very slowly. Mannie and I got a birch tree for the fire, but had a bit of bother with it.

January 15th Wednesday

Got up about eight, gave the cows a bit of hay, then had my breakfast. Milked, and fed the calves and pig. As it was raining, I was not able to do a deal outside. Manny has been at home today, as he thought it was no use going [to Keldy] as it was rainy. In the afternoon, Tom borrowed Milestone's cross-cut saw and sawed some birch trees down in the "bottoms", one out of the bank fence, as well.

I wrote an application to the railway company at York as porter. It has been thawing today and has almost got all the snow away, but was cold and wet.

January 16th Thursday

Got up about seven, foddered and milked before breakfast. Afterwards I fed the calves and pig. I turned the cows out for a run as it was a lovely morning. I got a dess of hay in and cleared up the rubbish around the stack. Tom has been to the station for a sack of Indian corn and a bag of maize which he ordered on Tuesday. Ernest Woodmancy came at darkening to get a bolt hole punched through a pair of cart arms which Tom did. Our folks have been washing. It looks like a change tonight, the snow is going fast.

January 17th Friday

Got up about seven and had my breakfast, then went out and foddered and milked the cows, while Tom was at the station with a basket for Jennie. Later I fed all up, then cleaned out the barn. I laid the door down in the yard for the getting in of the stack. After dinner we got a stack in, we have only one left. Tom and Mannie went to the station to get the basket, and got a form from the railway company for me to fill in. Mannie has not been at Keldy this week as the masons did not come. Hannah intended going tonight, but put off till morning. We went over to the bandroom and had a good practice, the first since Christmas. Mannie gave a few notes.

January 18th Saturday

Got up about eight, got my breakfast, then I had a lot of bothering about after Hannah, as she was going to Brewer's by the 10 o'clock train. Tom set her to the train and went to Newton for a few shop things. As I got a very bad start, I was all the morning getting done up. After dinner, I got some hay in then went to the railway station to see about filling in my form for the railway. I did not get it filled in. We stayed at the station ever so long. Tom milked and such like. I fed the calves. Pollie has been baking. Dull day, like rain.

January 19th Sunday

Got up about nine. Foddered and milked before breakfast, after which I fed the calves. Went to the bandroom where there was a practice for learners, so Tom did not go. There was only us four learners and the Piersons. Tom went out for his dinner and tea. I did not go to Stape at night as it was rather wet. A.Nicholes has gone onto the tenor, and I am using his cornet, and D.Holliday is playing bass. Mannie and I had a practice this afternoon, he gets on very well. I think it will be a thaw tonight.

January 20th Monday

Got up about seven, foddered and milked, then got all fed up. Went with the horse for some sticks from the trees which our folks call the birches, which Tom felled last week. I got ready after dinner intending going to Pickering for a reference for the N.E.R., but I was too long getting ready, so went over to Levisham and got a reference from Mr Armstrong. I went to Pickering on the twenty to five. I went to Major Mitchel's, but he was bad in bed, so I did not get one there. Went to two others, who were both out, at last went to Arthur Kitchen and got one. Fine morning, wet afternoon.

January 21st Tuesday

Did not get up till about seven, then foddered and milked and fed all up. About dinnertime, I went to Keldy to get a reference from Ernest Hill, and I got one.

Then I came home and got my tea, then went down to the station with the references. Old Mr Rymer [Levisham station-master] was in a nasty mood, so did not attend to them. Ernest Woodmancy came to get some stays made for his cart. Tom went with him and, while cupling[?] some iron, a chisel flew at the stable lamp and broke the glass. it has been a wet day and has got most of the snow away now.

January 22nd Wednesday

Up about half past seven. Went and gave the cows some fodder, then milked, and Tom separated whilst I had my breakfast. Then I was feeding all up and such like jobs till dinnertime. After dinner, Tom started to lead manure into the haystack field, the second half day this year, as he was leading manure half a day in the bank. At night Tom and Mannie went to Baker's to have a singing practice but John was not in. It has started to snow tonight and is very cold, but I hope it will not last long.

January 23rd Thursday

Up about seven, got breakfast, then went and foddered the cows and milked, then fed the calves. Went down the wood for some stakes to put some wire round the stacks to prevent the geese pulling straw out. I got my dinner before I put it up, then I gathered a sled load of wet rubbish that was about the stacks, and tied the sled beyond the cart, as Tom was loading manure.Our folks have been churning today. I wrote a letter to Jennie. Tonight we had Mr Pashby a bit. It has been much warmer today, the bit of snow has thawed.

January 24th Friday

Up about seven, had breakfast before I went out. Tom was at the station with the basket. Then I foddered and milked. After, I set a rig stick for Tom in the top of the second field, and also led the horse while Tom set it. Came on rain, so we did not get much ploughed. We borrowed Milestone's crosscut saw and sawed a few tree trunks up which we had at home. I brought the cows in and cut some chop and foddered them. At night, we went across to the bandroom. I left the milking till we came back, then mother said we might as well leave it till morning, and we did. Wet day, but nice and warm.

January 25th Saturday

Got up at seven, foddered and milked, then I was doing all sorts till dinnertime. Then I started to scrape up some of the mud on the highroad and about the bank gate. Swilled the yard and took out all the mud. Tom milked and did all up outside, while I got ready and washed the kitchen and dairy floors. Mannie went to Pickering and bought us a new stable lamp glass, also one for the house lamp. Fine day, freezing.

January 26th Sunday

Got up about nine, then foddered and milked before breakfast. Helped Pollie to straighten up for the meeting, as it is at our house today. George Holliday preached and also Mr Temple. The preachers stayed for their tea. Tom and I went to Stape chapel, and got inside, as well. Harold Nicholes and I were outside pimping. All is frozen up today and it is freezing keen tonight, but it has been a lovely fine day. Mannie milked for us at night.

January 27th Monday

Got up about 7.30am, foddered and milked, then fed the calves. I yoked up and led a bit of manure. Jennie came by the ten train and went back on the three o'clock, I set her to the station. Tom has been cutting ling. Mr Rymer has got word from the N.E.R. that they do not take youths under twenty as men porters. We all three went to Mr Baker's at night to have a sing, and we stayed there till after ten. It has been a fine day, but looks like rain tonight. One of our old ewes died.

January 28th Tuesday

Up about eight. then foddered and milked before breakfast . Tom went to cut ling and I stayed at home and got all done up. I brought a bag of potatoes in, then went with the horse and cart for a load of ling, also took Tom a bit of something to eat. When I got back, I had dinner then went back and brought all the lot down. We put it in the shop. It came on a very wet night. I did not go to the bandroom, as it was too wet. I have not been able to give the cows any chop as we have used up all the bran. Cold day, wet and stormy night.

January 29th Wednesday

We did not get up till late, as it was an awful dull morning. I foddered, then had breakfast. I got all fed up, then went and brayed round an ash stick. Had dinner , after which I cut some chop and mixed it for the cows, and got them in. I got all done up and had a sit down about eight. Pollie has been doing a bit of baking tonight. Tom and Mannie have been skinning the old sheep. Tom has been at Newton for some bran and meal. Mannie has been at Keldy. It has been a dull day and wet. I am going to bed at 10.30pm.

January 30th Thursday

We did not get up very soon, but we foddered and milked before breakfast. After, I cut some chop, and dug a hole for the old ewe. Tom helped me to put her in. After dinner, Tom borrowed Milestone's saw. I got the horse and cart and went for some trees - some of the remains of "The Birches" - and sawed them up. I wrote a letter to the railway company to say I would take any post that is vacant. I took it to the station and posted it. Came on a storm about five o'clock, but rain not snow. Very foggy and wet at night.

January 31st Friday

Got up a little sooner as Tom had to go to the station with the basket. I milked and fed all up, then I cut a big heap of chop till dinnertime, and put a swing in the barn for the children. After dinner, I helped Tom to make besoms. I stayed till about four o'clock, then he went to the station for the basket while I got the cows in and such like. The cows have been at the haystack and made a nasty going-on, but I cleaned it up as best I could. It came on a wet sort of night, so we did not go to the bandroom.

February 1st Saturday

We got up about seven or so, then Tom and I milked and got the calves fed and such like. I went to help Tom to make besoms and stayed with him till dinnertime. After dinner, Mannie was with him, so I got some hay in and chopped for Sunday. They went to Newton about 5pm for some paraffin, and brought a letter from the railway company which had been left at Pashby's. They do not want anyone just now. Got a letter from Hannah. It has been a cold day but not wet.

February 2nd Sunday

Did not get up till half past eight, as I sat up with Polly till past twelve, so no wonder Tom did all the milking and things outside this morning and I did all at night. Manny was talking of going to put a fire in Saintoft Cottage, but did not get off. I did not get over to Stape at night, but Tom went. We have run short of eatables so mother has had to bake a few cakes over the fire as Polly was too sleepy. I saw a very beautiful star over Rockly way tonight, it looked very big and bright. Very cold and wet at morning, better pm.

February 3rd Monday

Got up about seven, milked and got all done up, then started to bray ash as Tom wanted a lot of laps.

He had to go to Newton for flour first thing as we had nothing to eat. I cleaned the horse and pig out, and swept from the water trough to the stable door. I did not get a lot of laps off but plenty to keep Tom going. We have got all the sticks burned that we got last Thursday. Polly has been baking today, she used two stone of flour. Mother has a gathering on her foot and is not able to get about much. Fine day, few showers.

February 4th Tuesday

Got up about six, packed the besoms in the cart while Tom sawed them off at the "laps". We just got nicely ready for going when Mrs Baker came by and told us that all the shops in Pickering were going to close at eleven, so Tom thought it was no use going. He made some more, four dozen, I think. I went and pulled a few sheaves out of the last remaining stack as we have used all the other. Also got some hay in. We all three went to the bandroom at night and came away at 9o'clock prompt. Very fine day.

February 5th Wednesday

Tom got up a bit before me. I got up about seven and packed four dozen besoms on the cart, making twenty dozen. I helped Tom get off, then came and milked the cows and had some breakfast. After I fed all up, I was doing about the home. Spread some wet bedding out to dry. Went for a few potatoes for dinner and put them on. After dinner, I got a stick for the fire and got some sheaves in from the stack and some hay. Tom arrived back about six, then went to see Eddons about leading some straw from Mickel [?]Hicks. Fine day.

February 6th Thursday

Up about seven. Tom went to work at Keath's, so I was by myself today. I did not do much at morning except feed up and such like, but after dinner I started to lead manure. I intended going over to the bandroom, but did not get done up soon enough. We had a letter from Jennie saying she would be coming down on Saturday, and I sent Hannah a parcel with John Fletcher. Polly has been churning and baking today, though she didn't bake much as she hadn't much baking powder. Fine day, wet night.

February 7th Friday

Got up about seven, foddered and milked and got all done up, but not till about dinner time, as I took the basket to the station. Tom did not come home last night. I intended to lead manure after dinner, but it started to rain and kept at it till nearly night. Then there came a most tremendous gale. I thought would blow the stacks over, so I put a lot of rails on the haystack and a gate and left it as I could do no good, but I expect to see it blown over in the morning, but I hope it won't. I was down for the basket at night, saw Florrie Gibson.

February 8th Saturday

Up about seven, looked at the stacks and was surprised to find that the wind had done them no harm. I did all up then got a bag of potatoes in. Cleaned out the horse and cows. After dinner, when Manny came home, we went and got half *of the corn stack in, it is the last one we have. Then went out into the Yewfells for a snigging of sticks. Jennie came by the four o'clock train. I cut the chop for Sunday, and foddered all up, but not till late. Tom came home tonight about ten.*

February 9th Sunday

Up about nine, foddered and milked and got all fed up before breakfast, but it was eleven before I got it. I went to the bandroom. I played a few hymns in the lead, as Tom was foddering the stock. When I came back, I turned the cows out and got dinner, then I had a bit of a read. I foddered all up at night, then went over to Stape, but I did not get there till eight. Mr Temple has been preaching tonight. Tom and Manny were over at the Saintoft cottage today. Tom and Manny have done nothing today. Very fine and warm.

February 10th Monday

We did not get up very soon as it was a wet morning. It faired up and Tom went with the horse for the straw, and I went and mended Fletcher's lane for them, but they did not come back, they left the wagon load of straw at Stape. Jenny went away with the 3 o'clock train. Polly got a baby boy tonight, born a bit after nine, so we had a bit of a bustle on. Mrs Milestone came to help. Mr Temple gave his finishing address tonight, he has got no converts this time. Been dull and damp.

February 11th Tuesday

Got up about half past six. I was going to work at Levisham, but I had no shoes to go in. I had a bit of house work to do this morning. Tom went with the horse for the straw. Eddons brought one of their horses as well, John William and Jack came with it. It seem very good straw. Tom and I fenced round the stacks. Tom went into Pickering at night to do a bit of business. Jenny came back with the 8 o'clock train, we shall be alright now. Misty morning, very fine afternoon.

February 12th Wednesday

Got up about half past six, got a drink of tea and went to Keath's instead of Tom, went in Tom's shoes. William was in the sheepfold when I arrived so I went and helped him to set a net or two and pulled a few turnips. Then we got the horse and cart and lead them into the cow pasture for the sheep in lambing time. After dinner, William and I got a small round pyke in for chopping purposes. I came home at night. All are getting on favourably, the doctor was up today, also Mr Marsden. It has been a very fine day.

February 13th Thursday

I got up about half past six and intended to go to Levisham, but, as it was getting a bit late, I stayed at home. I foddered and milked. Ted Hardcastle came to make a couple of gates for Keldy, and I went to show him where they were wanted. I went to the station to see if the wagon of coke had come in for the Keaths, as I would have gone to help them to lead it if it had. I went to lead manure during the afternoon. Tom has been doing a bit of gardening today. Very fine day.

February 14th Friday

Up about six, then got breakfast and went with Jennie's basket to the station, as she was away on the 8am train. I went to work at Levisham. Old Ned and I were ploughing in the big field all day. I stayed at night. We have been ploughing seed. At night, I was down at the reading room. It has been a very fine day, but has come on misty and damp tonight. We only had a half meat pie warmed up for our dinner, and not very fresh at that.

February 15th Saturday

Got up a bit before six. I cleaned out the cows and brushed three horses over before breakfast. Then we set off to plough. I had a fur to take up, and Ned a rig to set. The train brought some coke in for Keaths, so we had to go for some of it. They would not let us into the station as the gate was locked, but we got in with a bit of shouting. It was rather late when we got them emptied. I had to help with the horses at night, as Ned went away.

February 16th Sunday

I did not get up till about nine, then did a few things around the house. We went to the bandroom and had a good practice. Matt came up this afternoon and Tom and I went with him round the fields, but he did not come into the house. Polly has got up a bit today. I went to Stape at night, I did not go to Stape when I intended, but went and sat reading in the parlour. We are nearly out of provisions. Fine day.

February 17th Monday

Got up at half past five, got a bit of breakfast, then set off to Keaths. We were leading the remainder of the coke from the station. Got it all brought up, but did not get it unloaded till dark.

February 18th Tuesday

Got up at half past five. Cleaned the cows out and brushed my pair of horses over. Got breakfast, then went to plough in the seed field. Was ploughing all day. Went to the reading room at night. Been a fine day.

February 19th Wednesday

Got up at half past five. Cleaned the cows out and got the horses ready, then Ned and I went to plough. After dinner, I had to help William to get some hay in, it was very windy and made it awkward to load.

February 20th Thursday

Was ploughing all day. I did not take my diary with me this week, so I have a lot of back reckoning to do, and I have forgotten what I was busy with most days.

February 21st Friday

Got up about five and, when I went to the cow house, I found a calf in the grip. It seemed all right, so I put it in an empty stall, and cleaned out and went to plough, but when we came home at dinnertime, they said it had been bleeding at the navel and was almost dead. They have got it stopped. Old Jane seems to think that we had pulled it with is navel fast to the cleansing. We have been ploughing all day.

February 22nd Saturday

Got up about half past five, cleaned out the cow house and brushed and geared my pair of horses for the plough, then, after breakfast, we went to plough. We were ploughing till dinnertime, then I had to stay and help kill the pig. I was leading a bit of manure onto the ..[?].. and the bay mare did not like the smell of the blood, so had to loose her out while I filled the cart. Stabled at night as Ned had to go to the train. Went home. Hannah has not come home yet from Brewer's. Fine day.

February 23rd Sunday

I did not get up very soon and did not do much work, except a few odd jobs in the house. I lit Polly a fire in the parlour and such like. I did not go to the band room, but Tom did. Manny went out a while at night. We straightened up, *thinking it was our night meeting, but no one came. We did not go to Stape at night, because it was too late for chapel by we got milked. Polly has been up all day, but has a headache. Fine day.*

February 24th Monday

Did not get up till about seven, then helped Tom with foddering and such like, then he went to Pickering with the one o'clock train to see Dobson's sale. I borrowed Fred Milestone's bicycle pump and got ready and went to Pickering on the bike about five o'clock. I had an insurance card to get and nine stamps to put on, also got measured for a pair of boots from Mr Blacklock. Went to Polly Milestone for some tea. Set off back about half nine, got to Newton at ten. Fine day.

February 25th Tuesday

Got up about half past six, had a bit of breakfast, then set off to Keath's. When I got there, I cleaned my pair of horses, had some more breakfast, then went with old Ned to plough in the big seed field. I was ploughing all day. Keath's calf seems to be getting better. Old Jane has been baking, and having some pain in her head. We went to the reading room at night. It has been a fine day, but cold. I am going to bed at about ten. I think there is nothing very important today.

February 26th Wednesday

Up about half past five, mucked out and foddered, then brushed my pair of horses for the plough, then, after breakfast, Ned and I went to plough. I did not go to plough in the afternoon, as William and I went to the field for a load of hay, then we set the engine on and made some chop - she went very well. We had Jane pulling [?] the chop by and I cutting sheaves. I milked for William as he had to go to church. Went to the reading room at night. Fine day, but dull.

February 27th Thursday

Up at half past five, cleaned the cows out, then brushed the horses over and went to plough. It started to rain in the morning. We were ploughing the seed field headlands, then came to the howe field in the afternoon. It was raining all day and made it very nasty working. I went to the reading room at night. Robinsons have been asking for one of us to go to thrash there tomorrow if it is fine.

February 28th Friday

Got up about half past five. As we had only one match, we had lit the candle about four, and it had to keep burning or we could not have lit it again. I cleaned the cows out and got my horses ready for the plough and got as far as the limekiln field gate, when we saw that Robinsons were on thrashing. So I had to come back and go to help them, as William was busy and could not go. I was carrying corn, the first time I have. William went at the afternoon, and Ned and I went to plough. Been snowy showers all day.

March 1st Saturday

Got up at half past five. old Ned was bad during the night with a cold. I did my usual jobs, then Ned and I went to plough in howe field. I was almost starved to death, it was so cold. After dinner, we went and brought the engine and thrasher out of Robinson's high yard. We had not much bother with her, only a bit of backing of the engine to get turned out of Robinson's yard. I was leading turnips into the cow pasture, also got a bit of hay in.

March 2nd Sunday

Did not go to bed last night till 2am, as Polly sat up working and I was reading the paper. It was after eight when I got up. Nursed the baby, then went to the band room. Tom did not go and Mannie went to Saintoft cottage to light a fire, he came back about seven o'clock. Polly has been bad all day with a sick headache, and I had to straighten up the house as it was our night meeting. Only Mr and Mrs Milestone and Frank Pickering came. Polly and I stayed in the parlour and we could not get the fire to burn. Did not get to Stape at night. Fine day, but rather cold.

March 3rd Monday

Did not get up till seven as I heard it was a wet morning. Helped Tom to milk and such like. It faired up about half past seven and I thought I would go to Keath's at dinnertime, as it was too late to go at morning. I helped William to water the cows. Got dinner , then went to plough. I had a fur to take up and a rig to set at the low side of the howe hill. Old Ned has not been today, so I have been by myself. Wet at morning, but fine afternoon.

March 4th Tuesday

I did not wake up this morning till half past six, so had to look sharp. I did not do anything at the cows, as Ned is off this week, he is bad with indigestion. I am acting the part of wagoner. I was helping William to tidy up for the thrashing. I scraped the mud up about the machine end. In the afternoon, we were thrashing, I was carrying straw, and it was very windy. We carried most of it into the barn. We have got thrashed out. Fine day.

March 5th Wednesday

Got up about half past five. Cleaned out the horses and gave them some straw for the day, as John Stead's were to be on thrashing. William and I went and we were both on jacking straw. I only had a little stacking fork. It was a bit windy. We did not get a very good start in the morning on account of the engine not having her steam up, and got done about four. Then I did the cows and horses before supper. Fine day, rather windy.

March 6th Thursday

Got up about half past five, went and fed the horses and cleaned them out. Then had breakfast and gave the horses that were staying some more straw. I went to plough with Bonnie and Jet. I had to plough round the old howe hill this morning, I got it done very well. In the afternoon, I took the other pair. There was a boy came who wanted hiring, and William engaged him, he is coming on Monday. Fine, cold day, wet at night.

March 7th Friday

Did not wake up till I heard William go past my chamber door about six. I did the horses and went to plough. I had a fur to take up and a rig to set along the limekiln field side, a half moon shape. After dinner, we had five quarters of barley to put up for Arthur Duesbury then we went to the station with four horses and the cart for some chippings for the footpaths. We only had time for one load, put them along Wimbush's wall side.

March 8th Saturday

Up about half past five, did the horses and such like, then, after breakfast, I went to plough. It was rather a cold job first thing at the plough. I took the other pair of horses at the afternoon. William asked me to stay all night, as they have a cow due to calve and perhaps would need a little help. So I went to the station at night to tell some of our people, if they should have been down, that I would not be coming tonight. I met Tom bringing Dale's some besoms so came back with him. Fine day, showers afternoon.

March 9th Sunday

I did not come home last night, as William had a cow due to calf, but it did not come off. I went to the bandroom with Tom. It was our meeting and we had a great fuss on. Tom and Mannie went over to Saintoft to make a fire. Frank and George Pickering were the preachers. I went to Stape at night, got into the chapel, heard old Ainsley preach. It was a very wet, dark night, so we came over by Pierson's to borrow a light.

March 10th Monday

Up about half past five, got a bit of breakfast, then went over to Levisham. Old Rickinson came and wanted the rest of the chippings bringing up. I went with three horses and a cart as the wagon would have been too heavy and clumsy. We led them to the whin corner and threw them onto the road. We also put some on George Stead's field and a few up the wood. Brought one load to Levisham. The new wagoner came at dinnertime. Finished leading about three, then led a bit of manure. Fine day.

March 11th Tuesday

Up at half past five, did the horses while the boy did the cows. Got them ready and went to plough. Was ploughing the last throwing out piece. After dinner, we ploughed the headlands, then brought our ploughs home and yoked into the cart and led a bit of manure into the pond field. We had Diamond and Jet and we stuck fast half way up the field and had a bit of it to throw off. It has been a fine day, but cold.

March 12th Wednesday

Got up about ten minutes to six, worked among the horses till breakfast, then went to harrow in the seed field, or big field, but it had been a keen white frost and the harrows would not penetrate it at all, so we loosed out and came home and started to lead manure onto the pond field. After dinner, we went to harrow again, and it worked beautifully. I had the old lame mare and Diamond in the three chisel harows, and the boy had the small harrow with the other pair of horses. It has been a fine day but cold.

March 13th Thursday

Got up at half past five, got worked up then, after breakfast, we went to harrow. It had been a bit of a frost, but nothing to do us any harm. I took one chisel harrow off, as it was a bit over hard work for the horses to have to pull three chisel harrows. we finished the field about four in the afternoon, then came into the howe field and it harrowed very well. Most people are on sowing now. It was a lovely morning but looks like rain tonight.

March 14th Friday

Up at half past five. Did all up then, after breakfast, went to harrow in the howe field. We finished it in the morning. After dinner, we took our ploughs and went to the bull field to plough, as it is all to do except or a bit at the top end. I set two rigs and we had one each, as we ploughed it cross-over. William went to Dick Holtby's sale at Stape but did not buy anything. It has been raw and cold today and looks like coming on some wet tonight.

March 15th Saturday

When we got up this morning it was white over with snow and had been a heavy frost, so we could not go to plough. We started to clean out the old mare's box, and then we cleaned out the other next to it, yoked three horses into the wagon and led it away. We were leading all day, as William cleaned the foal out and the other box where he had had a pig. I am not going home tonight as it is wet.

March 16th Sunday

Did not get up till seven, then we cleaned out the horses. We finished by breakfast time, then I came home. Got a wash, changed my shirt and went to the bandroom. Tom did not go as he had not done all up. After dinner, Tom, Hannah, Frances and I went to Milestone's meeting, Billy Scales was preaching. We also went to Stape at night, only Tom and I got into the chapel. Bob Smiddy was preaching. It has been a cold day, but has kept fine.

March 17th Monday

Up about half past five, got a bit of something to eat and went to Levisham. We went to plough this morning in the bull field. It started to snow and kept coming showers all the forenoon. It was rather cold too, but we got a bit of shelter behind the far side hedge. We set off back after dinner, but it started to snow again, so we turned back. We started to winder some oats, but the old fan did not go very well, so we were bothered a bit putting her right. It has come on a frost tonight, so it will make it very slape.

March 18th Tuesday

When we looked out this morning all was white over with snow and there had been a very hard frost, so we were not able to work the horses. We were windering again, did a few oats, then took the fan into the other end and started among the barley. The sun got out about dinnertime so we were able to go to plough in the afternoon. I set a fresh rig towards night. It only blew a little cold and it looks like coming some more snow. Was down at the reading room at night. I saw a dandelion in bloom on the bull field hedgeside.

March 19th Wednesday

Got up about half five and it was raining and pouring down, a regular storm, so we went in the granary and were on windering barley till about ten. Then it faired up, so we went to lead manure with the wagon and four horses. In the afternoon, we went to plough and it was very windy and cold. A man from York was here this afternoon putting the oil engine right. We were doing a bit of choping during the dinner hour. It is a good moonlit night.

March 20th Thursday

Up at half past five, did my horses and, after breakfast, we went to plough, we were ploughing all day. It came on like rain around dinnertime, but it blew off again, although it was rather showery all day. We are almost ploughed up to the nets. Hannah has been over helping Miss Keath today. I do not know whether we shall have a holiday tomorrow or not, but perhaps we shall not yoke the horses. It has been a fine day on the whole. Was down at the reading room at night and there is awful dozy doing down there.

March 21st Friday (Good Friday)

Got up at half past five, did the horses, and William said he should not use them today, so we set on to sweep up the yard. After dinner, we were shovelling up the stackyard. I went over to Stape at night as there was to be an entertainment in the chapel and a supper afterwards. It started at half past six and I did not set off from here till quarter to six, but I got in. It rained and poured down as I went and I got wet through at the knee. I came back to Levisham with Reg.

March 22nd Saturday

Got up about half past five, did the horses and, after breakfast, we went to plough. I had a rig to set when William got the turnips pulled out of my way. We have been ploughing all day, have the last rig set across the top and which has been ploughed over before, so it is like quarting. I expect that John Watson and Jane Holliday will have got married today. It came on a thunderstorm after we got down to the reading room. I am not going over home as it is a wet night.

March 23rd Sunday

Got up at half past six, started the horses and finished them after breakfast. Got washed and dressed and went to church. After church, I came across home. Did not get far as it has been a very wet day. I went to Stape, but did not get into the chapel. Tommy Brewer has been here for the day, he is staying for the weekend. Duke also came down from Fletchers and is staying for the afternoon. It has been a very wet day, was snowing this morning, then small stuff all day.

March 24th Monday [Easter Monday]

Up about half past five, got some breakfast, then went to Levisham. The boy and I were ploughing all morning, and we went back again, but I thought that Bonny looked like foaling, so I sent him home. I stayed and took a fur up and then I set the headland mark round the field. It has been a fine day. Old Ned has not landed yet. I got here this morning about seven. Thomas William Brewer was going to thrash at Newton, our people do not expect him coming back tonight. I am going to bed about ten. William is sitting up with the mare.

March 25th Tuesday

Jane came shouting about eleven last night that the mare was foaling, so I had to get up. It had foaled when I got out, we were trying to get it to the pap till 3 o'clock in the morning, then I went to bed, but William stayed with her till daylight. The mare seems to take to it alright, but it won't suck, and is bunged up in its inside, and we have given it two or three doses of physic. Old Willie Hurt came down at night and got it to suck. I have been ploughing the headland and got it finished, then came into the pond field.

March 26th Wednesday

Jane came shouting about eleven last night, as the mare was bad with colic. We got a bottle of colic mixture into her but it did not do any good. She was something awful in pain all the night. William and I were in the box with her all night and a cold, nasty job it was, too. As soon as it was light in the morning, I went and borrowed Frank Stead's bicycle and went to Pickering for Blench. He was going out so he did not come till dinnertime, when he gave her some medicine, but said that she would not get better. She died about seven at night. I was with her all the afternoon and we fomented her with blankets. Very fine day but cold.

March 27th Thursday

I did not get up till six as I was very sleepy and tired. I did the horses and, after breakfast, I went to plough in the pond field. After dinner, I got the horse and cart and took a couple of boxes to the station and brought some back. Took the two Jets and went to plough. Took a fur up and also set another ridge. Our folks have been looking for Ellerby coming for the mare, but he has not landed yet. William has sold a cow and calf today. The people about here have beeen sowing corn today. Fine day, but looks rather like coming wet.

March 28th Friday

Got up at half past five and did the horses. After breakfast, went to harrow in the big field, as the hill top took the straight set. It came on a regular storm after dinner, so was not able to get back to the field. We were hanging up bacon and doing a few more such like jobs. One of Ellerby's sons came for the old mare and we helped him to loaden her. Then I took old Diamond and gave him a bit of a pull up Lockton hill. Did not get back till seven, as it was very hard work for the horses. Jane has been to Pickering. Fine morning, but wet afternoon.

March 29th Saturday

Up at half past five, did the horses, then, after breakfast, William wanted the box cleaning out where the mare had been, so we all three set on and cleaned it out. Took us all morning, I whitened the top while the others did the rest. After dinner, we were going to sow corn but it started to look like rain, so we went to lead thorns, instead. Got one load from the bottom of Swallowdale and took it to the church field. I loaded them. It came wet before we got the load down, and kept at it, and thunder about at half past seven. I shall stay all night if it keeps raining.

March 30th Sunday

Got up about half past six and did the horses. It came on wet, so I sat down for a while and had a read. About ten, it faired up, so I came on home. I had my dinner, then dressed and went with Hannah to Saintoft to see Polly. We stayed till about nine, came home. Borrowed Mannie's bicycle lamp to show us the road home, as it was rather dark. Wet morning, fine afternoon. All our people seem fairly well.

March 31st Monday

Up about five and made the fire, then Hannah made my breakfast and I went to Levisham. Arrived about a quarter to seven. We all three went for a load of thorns out of Swallowdale. Took them into the far field on the level wood bottom and it was fit to bog us. After dinner, we went to drill corn in the big field. I led the drill, it is the first time that I have led one. Got a rather crooked mark, but not bad for a start. Drilled five acre. Fine day, misty at morning.

April 1st Tuesday

Got up at half past five, did the horses, then, after breakfast, we yoked two horses into the cart and went to the hill top field and started to drill. We had John Stead's horse yesterday and again today. She went in the harrows but, after dinner, I put her in the drill instead of Jet. It came on wet about four o'clock and, my word, it fairly poured down. We loosed out and gathered the bags up in the cart and came home, almost drenched. We had the oil engine on after we came home. The foal died tonight, about seven.

April 2nd Wednesday

Up at the usual time, got done up, then started to clean out the foldyard with three horses and the cart, as the land was too wet to work. William was away at the conference at Malton. We finished the foldyard about three, so took a load or two off the manure heap and put them in a heap in the limekiln field bottom, opposite the limekiln, ready for potatoes in the pond field. We got two lambs today, the first we have had, but there are a good many now in the village. Very fine day.

April 3rd Thursday

Did not get up till about six, then did the work among the horses. After breakfast, we went to drill. We finished the field off this morning, but not till *dinnertime, as we had a lot of gays to run off the bottom end. We shifted into the howe field, got once round the headland before dinner. We finished it this afternoon and took the drill back, but it took us till about seven o'clock to get it done. We had one of John Stead's horses. I had Diamond and lame Jet on the drill, and they went away very well. Our Hannah has been here today. Very fine, warm day.*

April 4th Friday

Up at half past five, got done up, then the boy and I went and shifted the harrow from the howe field to the bull field. I started to chisel harrow with three horses, it was very hard so I had to put a stone on each harrow to make them go in. I got it done over once, then started to do it over again, but did not get it finished. The foxhounds met at Levisham today. William is busy among the ewes and lambs, we have just got a nice start lambing. Very windy and cold.

April 5th Saturday

Up at half past five, got worked up, then went to harrow again in the bull field. I finished it off for the second time over, and harrowed the headlands up, then it was dinnertime. After dinner, I was harrowing it the length way on, but with the same harrows. I broke the three horse cobble tree yesterday, so we borrowed one of John Stead's, and, today, I broke in two the piece of iron where the cobble tree fastens onto the harrow boak, but I got a piece of chain and it does for the purpose all right. I am going home tonight. Very windy and cold.

April 6th Sunday

Got up at half past six, made the fire, cut a bit of chop for the cows, then cleaned them out , milked and separated. Ater breakfast, I washed and changed my dirty shirt, got ready and went to the bandroom. I was playing a bit of lead, as Piersons were helping Bob Gibson to get his mares up. After dinner, I did not go anywhere, was playing the cornet and the melodeon. At night, I went over to Stape, but I was too late for the service. Very windy and cold.

April 7th Monday

Got up about half past five, but mother was mending my breeches, so did not get ready before six, then I got a drink and a piece of cake, and went to Levisham. They had gone to their breakfasts when I got there, so I had to manage till dinnertime with what I had. I went to harrow in the bull field, got it harrowed over, then I went to roll it with John Stead's flat roller. I did not get it done, but very nearly so. It was windy this morning and kept coming on showers of snow and sleet. I was working in my top coat all morning, and nearly starved to death, at that. The wind has settled towards night.

April 8th Tuesday

Got up about six, as we were a bit sleepy this morning. When we got all done up, I went to finish rolling the bull field, it took me nearly till dinnertime. I brought the roller and took her back, then watered and foddered the horse. In the afternoon, we went to sow. I went for the drill and Alf took the seed up with lame Jet. We got four bags of seed sown, which was about four acre. I was drilling by myself for most of the time, as William was busy among the sheep, but the land was in good fettle, so did not need anyone. I was working in my top coat this afternoon, as it was cold and wet. It was windy again this morning and has kept coming showers of cold soak.

April 9th Wednesday

Up about the usual time, got done up, then went to drill. Got it finished and took the drill back, it is the finish of our corn sowing for this year. The boy was harrowing with the lame mare. We were on chopping at dinnertime, and then went down into the west banks along the back lane for some sticks, which had been cut for us to make stakes of and such like. We were snigging them up into the lane. I had Diamond and the boy had lame Jet. We did not take the cart as William was not with us. I went to Lockton to get measured for a new working suit of corduroy. Cold, damp morning, but fine afternoon.

April 10th Thursday

Up at the usual time, did the horses, and then, after breakfast, we went to the wood for the rest of the sticks. We took the wagon with us and left her in the lane. William came on about dinnertime and helped us to loaden the wagon. We put them off down the stackyard. We went again in the afternoon and got the lot. William helped to loaden them, some of them were heavy beggars, too. We went down to the reading room tonight, as we haven't been before this week but once. It was roaking at morning, but better at afternoon.

April 11th Friday

Got up at half past five and did the horses. After breakfast, I went to quart in the pond field. It was a fine morning, but came in dull toward dinnertime. It started to come some very small snow. I went back after dinner. It was still snowing and gradually got worse and worse, till I was forced to loose out about four o'clock. I did not get wet as I had my top coat on. William was away at the consecration of Lockton cemetary. I was doing a bit of work sorting potatoes out till about half past five, then started to fodder up. We are not going down to the reading room tonight, but shall go and read in the house. Snowy day, about 4"deep.

April 12th Saturday

Got up at the usual time and did the horses then, as it was all covered with about six inches of snow, we could not get on with anything out with the horses, so went and cut some stakes out of the sticks we brought in the other day. We were working in the mouth of the low shed down the stackyard. I sawed them into five foot lengths, the boy dressed them, and William sharpened them. We were working down there all day, but without William in the afternoon. I am going to see if Simpson will cut my hair tonight, he said he would. Been a fine day.

April 13th Sunday

Got up about half past six, made the fire, but it did not burn very well. Did not do any work. Played a bit on the melodeon, then went with Tom to the bandroom. I did not go anywhere during the afternoon. Hannah went to Saintoft. I got ready at night to go to the chapel, when Tom came in and told us that he had seen Frank Pickering, who had told him that it was to be our night meeting , so I had to be sharp and get the house ready. I have a gathering coming on my thumb, have had a poultice on it tonight. Fine day.

April 14th Monday

Got up about five, did not bother to make the fire, nor anything, but got ready and went to Levisham. We went to the station first with the wagon for some things for Tomlinsons, then went for some thorns,which Mr Welburn gave us, down to George Stead's low howmer as they were cut off from that side. William left us and went to Pickering, it was past one when we got our dinner. I took the thorns down against the church. When I got back, we went for a few thorns we had left in our Swallowdale. Dull day, my thumb is not better.

April 15th Tuesday

I was wakened last night, about twelve, by Jane calling for someone to come and help with the mare as she was foaling. We had to take the young horse out of its box and we got her into it. The foal had got almost dry before we got the mare shifted and she would not take notice of it at all. William and I stayed with her till morning, then I went to plough. I was ploughing all day, no, not all day, as we were rowing on with the foal in the morning , as the mare won't take to him, bites and kicks whenever he comes near. Fine day, but wet at night.

April 16th Wednesday

It was a wet morning and we did not get on with much work. I suckled the foal at morning and then was sawing a few stakes as well as my thumb would allow, as it is getting worse. It is swollen up nearly the whole length of my thumb, so I thought that I had better go to the doctor. Came home about twelve and had to rush in a very great hurry to catch the one o'clock train. I took my Sunday shoes to get mended at Blacklock's. I went to Dr Murphy's with my thumb and he let it out, I had to get some cotton wool from the chemist's to wrap it up. Wet morning, fine afternoon.

April 17th Thursday

We did not get up till about seven. I had a bit of bother to get the cotton wool off my thumb, as it was stuck in. Tom went to plough a bit during the morning, and I was picking potatoes after him. I got three pails full, put them on the roadside, and whilst we were at dinner, the cows came and got them! We just got yoked again in the afternoon and it came on wet, so we were forced to come home. I had to walk up the dale for some water-cress, but it is too young yet. I have put some zambuck on my thumb and have it in a sling. Showery.

April 18th Friday

We did not get up till seven, then I helped among the things, but did not do anything particular, as it was a wet morning. I went to plough about half past ten and Hannah was picking potatoes after me. We were only on about an hour when it came on a very nasty shower, so we came home and had dinner. We went to borrow the bill, with which to chop off the besoms, from the Smithie's in the wood. I was doing a bit more ploughing, set a rig up in the barley field hedge side. I went with the cart for some ling that Tom was cutting. Showery morning, fine afternoon.

April 19th Saturday

I did not get up till seven, though Tom was up before. I helped among the cows, then went to help Tom. I chopped the besom ends off while he packed, then he went to Pickering. He took the light cart and went by the dale, as he only had nine dozen besoms. I was cleaning out the yard, and there was a lot of muck in it, too. I then swilled it, also cleaned out the gutter on the highroad. Tom came back about six, he had not set off till eleven. Then he went to Saintoft to cut Mannie's hair, and he stayed all night. I have been able to milk a cow tonight. Fine day with showers.

April 20th Sunday

I did not get up till half past eight and I had all to do, was doing a bit of something till dinner-time, as I cleaned the stable and swept the yard end. Jane was up this morning. Tom came back about twelve. I got ready to go to the meeting, but did not get off. We went to Stape at night and managed to get into the chapel. Our folks have got eight goslings out of nine eggs, so they have done all right. I called a bit at Baker's as I came from the chapel. It is a grand moonlit night, been a very fine day.

April 21st Monday

I got up about half past seven. Cleaned out the cows, then was doing a bit of aught till about half past ten, when we went to sow. I was harrowing and Tom was sowing. I was harrowing all afternoon, did it twice over with the chisel tooth harrow, then three times over with the straight tooth one. I went over to the Keaths at night to see how they were getting on and to see how many days they could spare me to help Tom. I have to go over either Thursday or Friday. I did not get back till twelve. We have sown the high side of the haystack field. Fine day after a rather damp morning.

April 22nd Tuesday

Got up about eight as I was awfully tired and had a very nasty headache, but it worked off during the morning. Tom went to Newton for some seed oats from Job's and a bit of rye from Creaser's. I got a potato pie in and did a few more odd jobs while he was away. We went to sow after dinner in the third field. I only got it harrowed over twice with the chisel tooth harrow, then I got ready and went to hear Mr Harland in the Stape Wesleyan chapel lecture on America, and he was well worth going to hear. Been a fine, warm day.

April 23rd Wednesday

Up about seven, cleaned out the cows and the horse, then went down to Bolton's to say she could not come to work today as she was lame in her legs. I went to harrow this morning in the third field, also set a fire on in the lingey field, and when I went on, after dinner, it had got burnt into the wood, and had burnt the railings as it had gone through. Tom and I put it out, then Tom went to plough and I was gathering potatoes after him. James Pashby was up for his milk at night. Our folks have the old Irish [?] goose coming off, but only two are chipped yet. Been a very fine day. Heard the cuckoo this morning.

April 24th Thursday

Up at half past five, got ready and went to Levisham. William and I went down to the church to fence. We were fencing all morning, but were not able to get down after dinner, as Mr Blench came to cut our foal. He went to John Stead's first. We went down to help them, then they came to help us. We tailed the two-year old and cut the foal, then William and I buried Jet's foal, which died on Tuesday, then I cleaned out the box where they had been. I put the two-year old back in it and the one-year old into the other box. Been a very fine day.

April 25th Friday

Up at half past five, did the horses and, after breakfast, William and I went down to do some more fencing in the church field, and the boy went to plough. We have been fencing all day and have not got round yet. William brought a lamb down from the field tonight which had lost the use of its legs, it cannot stir them, and is just like a wooden lamb. We were trying to give it some milk, but it could not drink as it was jaw-locked. Was down at the reading room at night, but they were sat in the dark, and we made too much noise for them, so did not stay long. Fine day but wet at night.

April 26th Saturday

Got up about half past five and, after breakfast, the boy and I went with the cart and three horses for half a ton of cotton cake. When we got back, I helped clean up the yard and the boy went to plough. Mary Hammond got married this afternoon and all the people of Levisham are having a half day off, as the archbishop is coming to preach. At half past three, I came over home to get dresssed, then got back to hear the archbishop preach, but had to look sharp. Came home with James Pashby, almost switched. Dull, showery day.

April 27th Sunday

I did not get up very soon as I was awfully tired with walking so much yesterday. We went over to the bandroom and had a very good practice, but there was not a lot there. I did not go anywhere else, as it came on wet in the afternoon and was wetting at night. Tom went to Stape at night, so Hannah and I milked for him. I am feeling very stiff about my legs tonight. It will be with running across home yesterday, as it was almost two when I set off from Levisham, and was racing at night, but got nothing. Fine am, damp night.

April 28th Monday

Got up about five. Intended going over to Levisham, but Tom wanted me to help him with the sowing, so I stayed. He sowed the corn and I harrowed. We have sown the first field today, from the gap to the road. Tom went up on the high moor to cut ling, and Hannah was picking potatoes after me. Polly came over from Saintoft just after dinner, she intended going back but it came on a very wet night, so they had to stay. Manny came over from Keldy to help carry the children, he had to stay too. Fine day, but wet night.

April 29th Tuesday

Got up a bit after five, got ready and went to Levisham. We unloaded some straw they had got from John Stead yesterday then Alf Leng came to shoe our horses. While he shod them we cut some chop. Then we went to the station for some coals, as a truck is in for the Armstrong's. We took the cart, did not get back till about one. After dinner, we went with a wagon and a cart. Got the cart unloaded, but did not unload the wagon, as it was getting late, for we did not set off for the station till about three. Been a very fine day.

April 30th Wednesday

We did not get up till half past six, so we had to look handy. After breakfast, we went and emptied the wagon, as we had left her loaded the night before. Then we set off for the station. We had a bit of bother to get up with the wagon, as Jet would not pull, but loaded up all right at the finish. We had a few to bring during the afternoon, but not such big loads, we have got them up now and aren't sorry, either. I went down to the reading room at night. It has been a very fine day.

May 1st Thursday

Up at half past five and did the horses. After breakfast, I went to quart. It came on very much like rain at dinner-time but did not come to much. William took lame Jet to Newton to be shod, as she has lost her fore-feet shoes. As it looked like rain, I could not take the other Jet out for, if she got wet on her back, she might get cold. So the boy and I went to set a couple of nets down Swallowdale, as we are dividing it so that we can keep the howmer side for hay. Sandiman was here today and he had lame Jet. William has gone to church. Been a rather dull day.

May 2nd Friday

Up at half past five and did the horses. After breakfast I went to plough. I had a fur to take up and also set a rig. Our people have been gardening today. In the afternoon, I went to plough with the two Jets. It came on a few drops of rain about five and looked awfully black, so I loosed out and came home and did a bit of gardening till night. I did not go down to the reading room tonight, stayed at home and read the papers. Our Hannah has been over working today.

May 3rd Saturday

Up at half past five, got all worked up among the horses and, after breakfast, I went to plough. I had a rig to set first thing. I was ploughing again during the afternoon. I came home tonight. Came from the station with John Fletcher. I had a fur to take up the last thing before I left tonight. It has been a very fine day, but has come in cloudy and rather like rain. Our corn is mostly out now, and it is not as crooked as I expected. There is some equally as bad at Levisham this year.

May 4th Sunday

I woke up about six and got a paper and read till eight, then got up. We went over to the bandroom and had a very good practice. We had Joe down with the drum and most of the old hands except Baker. Tommy Webb came over to our house today and went to chapel with us. We got inside, but made rather too much noise for the preacher who told us to be quiet. I got home about half past nine or so. I went to Stape and got my bicycle pump, which was on Tom's bike in Tom Eddon's wagon shed. Been a fine day.

May 5th Monday

Got up about five and I got ready. I looked down the hill before I set off and saw an old fox. I called Tom up but the fox had got away by then. He got a hen yesterday morning. I came to Levisham and brought my cornet with me, as Tom is coming over tonight to have a practice. I went to quart in the morning. I had a rig to set first thing. After dinner, we had to go to the station to load manure (phosphate). We took the wagon to the hill top, then brought a cart-load and put on her. We put nine bags on from the station, which is not a bad load for three horses. We had a rousing band practice tonight. Fine day.

May 6th Tuesday

Got up at five and got the horses ready. After breakfast, went to the station for the rest of the manishment, also brought up an eight stone bag of calf meal which was at the station for us. We got it all up this morning, there was three and a half tons, got up in four loads. After dinner, it was raining, so we did not yoke the horses. Instead, we cleaned the calves out and got Jet shod, then did a bit of gardening during a fine fit. I did not take my top coat with me this morning and nearly got wet through, serves me right as it was roaking before I set off. Been a nasty, roakey day.

May 7th Wednesday

Got up a few minutes past five, prepared the horses ready for work, but William thought it was too wet to go to quart, so gave the horses some hay, and the boy and I went down to the garden to plant potatoes. It was rather wet, but did not do so bad. My word, there are some wicks in it, keeps you going picking them out, and there was still lots left when we had finished. I went to quart in the afternoon. It looked like rain and is very cold, but it kept fine this afternoon. I set another rig just before I left tonight, and a straight one too! Dull day, very cold.

May 8th Thursday

Up about five, got the horses done and ready for the plough. After breakfast, I went to plough. I got the piece rigged up before dinner. I took the other Jet and left lame Jet in, for Sandiman would be coming during the afternoon. It came on wet around four, I stayed for about an hour out then, as it seemed to get worse and I thought the mare might catch cold, I came home. I found an old King George coin whilst I was ploughing today, it is marked 1806. I went down in the cow shed to sharpen stakes to make up the night. Dull, cold day, wet night.

May 9th Friday

Got up about half past five. It was raining and pouring down, so could not get out with the horses. I went up into the granary and started to turn some heaps of barley. It took me nearly till dinner-time, then went and sharpened a few stakes till dinner. We have nearly got all our hay used, shall finish it today. William went to see if Simpson would let us have some - he would, so we went for it. Old Jane was in a rage when we got back because I had cut the Galloway's tail off. I went over to the old house for a band practice. They had all gone to bed when I got back to Levisham, so I got in among the hay and had a nice warm doss till six.

May 10th Saturday

I awoke first at half past four, went back to sleep till six, then got out of my hay bed. We thought it would be too wet on the land today, so we all three went down in the ing to fence. After dinner, I had to go to meet the three o'clock train with the cart to bring some luggage for the Tomlinsons. We were weighing hay up before I went. After I got back, I took the wagon and went to Welburn's for a load of straw. Johnny forked and I loaded. We got a nice bit on but it was all on one side. Had to be driven steady, but I landed up alright, and we unloaded it, which made us rather late. Came home. Fine day, looked like rain at pm.

May 11th Sunday

I did not get up very soon. Had breakfast, then I thought I would take Mr Pashby his milk down as he is away. I gave Tom my cornet to take over, so that I came up the slack to the bandroom. Tom had been gawping and lost my cornet mouthpiece and stem as he came over to the bandroom, and we cannot find it anywhere. It was our meeting this afternoon. The preacher came but did not stay for his tea. I was at Stape at night, got to the chapel. I have got Harry Holliday's cornet mouthpiece and stem to play with tomorrow. Was like thunder this afternoon, but passed off.

May 12th Monday [Whit Monday]

We did not get up very soon. I helped to milk, then did not do much of anything but clean my shoes and get ready for the 11o'clock train, as we are going to play at the picnic on the island at Egton Bridge. Tom made over he had to take the horse to get removed this morning. I had to look sharp to get the train. We started to play about two o'clock. We played the lancers seven or eight times and the quadrilles about three, besides the polkas and schottische and such like. There was a lot of people there. I walked back with Peirsons and Donie. Got home about one in the morning, plugged tired. Fine day, but misty.

May 13th Tuesday

I did not get up till half past eight, as I was sleepy. I helped to milk, then washed my feet and cut my toe nails. Read a bit till dinner was fit, and went to Levisham for the afternoon. I went to quart, I had a fur to take up and also a rig *to set up along the top wall side, so that I shall have the gays to come on in the throwing out piece. Alf Leng has been here for his supper and has been helping William to chop. I was down at the reading room at night. I think there is nothing very special today. Been a nice warm day, but dull at night.*

May 14th Wednesday

Got up at half past five, cleaned the stable out and fed and brushed the horses. After breakfast, I went to plough and the boy went to roll with John Stead's roller and Diamond in the big field. I got the bit rigged up to the wall, then had the gays to run off, which took me nearly half a day. Got them done about four, then set a rig up the limekiln field side, as I am going to rig the headlands up. I did not get it quite done. I went down to the station at night for my top coat, which I left when we went to Egton. Fine morning, cold and damp pm.

May 15th Thursday

Got up at half past five and got the horses ready. After breakfast, I went to plough the headland, then set a rig the other side. I did not get it done before dinner, finished it about four in the afternoon. I came down for the Cambridge roller, which was in the yard, and went to roll the limekiln fence side. I missed the headland out as it was not dry enough. I did not get very much done. I was down at the reading room at night, but could not read the papers as they had not got a light. Fine day, very cold at night.

May 16th Friday

Got up at half past five. Got the horses fed and ready for work, then I went and did a bit more rolling. It took me nearly till dinner-time to get half of it done, then I set a rig with the boy's plough, as it had the best sock. I was ploughing all the afternoon, but did not seem to get much done as I am ploughing it lengthway on. I started a bit off the headland. I did not go anywhere at night as John Stead's boy came up and we stayed talking. Our Hannah has been over here working today. I have been rather poorly today, sick and a headache, am feeling a little better now. Been a very fine day. Slept the cows out.

May 17th Saturday

Got up about a quarter past five and fed the horses. After breakfast, I went and got the digger out of the low shed and William helped me to get her into running order. I have got a nice bit more done now, as I can turn a lot over at a time. I set a fresh rig about dinner-time and have been ploughing to it this afternoon. William has been fencing down in the far ing. I am going to sleep the horses out tonight for the first time. We had a cow calved just before I took the horses out. I went home at night, was reading till late. William was out sheep lading. William gave me three shillings short, it is a mistake, but I shall let it pass, but it is a lot to look over. Been a very fine day.

May 18th Sunday

I did not get up till about half past eight as I sat up late last night. I had a bad headache again this morning, but it passed off towards night. Tom and I went to the bandroom. It seems that Tom found my cornet mouthpiece and stem somewhere against the lingey field wall sometime during the past week. He went to look for his sheep, which have been lost since lst Monday night. He found them at John Pierson's in Hartoft, all right and one of them had lambed. Bob Atkinson and his uncle came to see my father and stayed for tea. Went nowhere at night. Been a cold and showery day.

May 19th Monday

I got up about five or so and, as mother was up and had the fire made, I got some breakfast before I set off to Levisham. I was ploughing with the old digger. I got the rigging -up piece done this morning, and started to throw out after dinner. We had a good laugh at dinner-time, as William went to the station with Jane in the trap and we had our dinners alone. Had a cat hunt. I took the horses down to the bottoms at night. I was going to Lockton but decided to go tomorrow night. We have got all our stock out now except for a couple of new calven cows, which go out at days now. Cold and showery.

May 20th Tuesday

Got up at five and went for the horses. Went down with John Stead's boy. Our horses were bad to catch, but got them with a bit of bother. I went to finish the throwing out piece I was on with, then I started to roll it down, as the boy had been harrowing it with one horse and there were a good many clots. We set a few rows of potatoes alongside the tares. I made the rows with the old digger, and covered them up with her as well. They were not made as well as might have been expected, but not so bad for a first start, and a digger too. Cold day.

May 21st Wednesday

Got up at five. Took a bit of Robson's cake down with me to catch the horses and got them without the least bother. I was going to roll, but did a bit of harrowing instead. Then I started to to roll it cross-over at the top end, got about half way by dinner. I am going to do a bit of rolling up by the side of where I left off ploughing, as we shall not start to drill today, as intended, but wait till morning. We have got the land fit for the swedes half way across the field from the limekiln field fence, and I am going to start to work the other side now for yellowing. Fine am, wet pm.

May 22nd Thursday

Up about five, went for the horses and got them all right. I went to the field with the wagon and the manishment, and William brought the drill. We got on very well. Some of the rows had a bit of a twist in them, but all were passable for a man who hasn't drilled any before. Got drilled as far as we had land fit by dinner-time. We had three horses up and down. I am going to plough this afternoon. If I get done in good time tonight, I shall go over to Lockton to see about my clothes.[Written during dinner break]
I did not go to Lockton, as it was too late. Been a fine day.

May 23rd Friday

I did not get up till half past five, as I was out rather late last night with Frank Stead. I went to plough and it works beautifully, not a bit clotty as it was the other day. It is the rain that has done it. I was ploughing all day, got the rigging-up piece done and a start on the throwing-out piece. I was over at Lockton at night but Sedman has not got my things done yet. I came back with George Stead. I got an eighteen pence postal order to send to Mr Simpson, but have not sent it yet. I have got my Sunday suit paid for now when I get this sent. Our boy has bought Reg's bicycle. Hannah has been over today. Been a fine day.

May 24th Saturday

Up at half past five and went and got the horses and, after breakfast, I went to plough. I took Jet up to Pierson's horse at Robinson's at dinner-time, but she would not have any. The boy has been to the station with some luggage for Tomlinsons. This afternoon I got the throwing-out piece done and set a rig about *five yards from the wall up Robinson's cow pasture. I came home at night, arrived about nine, got to bed at half past ten. Our Tom is sleeping his cows out for the first time. Our folks had just milked when I got home. Been a very warm day.*

May 25th Sunday

Got up about six, read till eight, then had breakfast and helped Tom to milk. James Pashby came up and, after I had got a good wash, we all went up the fields. Tom and I went to the band room, we have been playing the new books this morning and had a good tune, but did not know them. I am going to Newton, to the Primitive anniversary, tonight. Hope I shall get a seat in the chapel.

I went to Newton but the chapel was full, so I had to stand in the doorway. The singing did not go so bad, but George Pickering did not do so well on the harmonium. Pollie and family came over at night, they are going to help to set potatoes. Been a grand, warm day.

May 26th Monday

Got up about half past four as mother thought the clock was half past five. I brushed and packed my old Sunday suit ready to take to Levisham, as I shall want it on Wednesday to go to Newton. Then got ready and went to Milestone's for my bicycle, as I am going to take her over with me to clean, as she is rusty, for Fred had not cleaned her since he had her at Pickering a few weeks ago. Got to Levisham and gave the dog a fright as I came in the yard. Went to plough in the morning, and was finishing off and doing a bit of digging during the afternoon. Fine day.

May 27th Tuesday

Got up about five and went for the horses. After breakfast, I took the three horses and started to drag the wall side as there are a few wicks from the pond to about the first hedge up from Robinson's cow pasture. They are all in a bed about twelve yards wide. I was rolling after I got the wicks dragged out. I did not get more than half the piece rolled before night. At night, I had a good go at cleaning the bike. I got her to look a bit better, but have not got her done all over yet. Have only got the front wheel done, the spokes take up a lot of time doing. Very hot in the morning, cooler at pm.

May 28th Wednesday

Got up at five, went for the horses, then went to harrow. I am going to harrow the piece over with the big chisel harrow. I did not start first thing, as I believe I was doing something else, but am not sure. I left a bit sooner tonight to go to Newton tea feast. Set off from Levisham with Frank Stead. I did not help the Stape band to play as I thought they had plenty without me. Landed home about eleven. Reg Masterman was with us when we came back. There was not much on at Newton. Fine day.

May 29th Thursday

Got up at the usual time at five and went for the horses. Went to finish off harrowing with the big chisel harrow. It took me till dinner-time to get it done. We were off to drill in the afternoon but it came on wet, and so William and I went for a grass reaper which William has bought off Arthur Estill of Newton. She is a Dearing Ideal. We came down the wood road to Sole Gate beck, then came on Raper road to the station. My word, what a road it is to bring a reaper, and it was sunny and warm, and it made us sweat very much as we had to hold her back over the ledges and stones. Got home safe with nothing lost or broken. I had a good go at the bike, got the hind wheel cleaned tonight.

May 30th Friday

Got up and went for the horses. After breakfast, we went to drill. I went up with the wagon with the manure. William borrowed the drill and I came back for her. We did not get a very straight line this morning as the boy led the first two horses very bad. We got all our yellow seed drilled by dinner-time, so we borrowed some soft seed to finish off with. We packed the wagon with the harrows and such like, and took them up to the five acre on the boak. It came on a thunder storm and we were caught in it as we came back, and I got wet through as I only had a smock on, so put one of William's shirts on. Very hot day, it burned my arms this morning while drilling.

May 31st Saturday

Got up as usual and went for the horses. After breakfast, I went to the five acre on the boak and started to harrow with the big chisel harow, as William thought she would cut a lot of rubbish as she was newly laid (the field is yellow over with brassocks and there are a lot of thistles too) but she did nothing of the sort as the ground was rather hard. So after dinner I was told I had better give it a drag over, but not with much better results, for there was as many left almost as there was when I started, but I kept on with it till night. I was going to go to Pickering on the bike, but it came on a wet night so had to stay at home. Hannah was over today.

June 1st Sunday

I did not get up till about eight, and did not do much as Tom and Mannie milked (Mannie and Pollie have been here a week helping Tom to set potatoes, they go home tomorrow). I got washed and dressed, as did Tom and Mannie, and we went over by the old house to take some music, and across to Keldy, as we wanted to have a look at how it was going on. They have got it built one storey high, it looks very nice. Then we went down the avenue and had a look at the fish-pond. Went on to Saintoft, made a fire and found a nest of eggs in the garden so we fried some and had a good dinner, there was plenty of eatables in the house. I went to Cropton to the Primitive Methodist anniversary. Came back with old Magson and Francis Stead, I saw Joe Harland and John Willie Dennis and a few others. Been a fine day.

June 2nd Monday

Up about five, got a bit of breakfast, then set off to Levisham. The boy had got the horses in, which he always does on a Monday morning as I haven't time. I went to plough in the five acre after breakfast. Set a rig with the little old plough then, as ahe didn't cut all the rubbish, I went and got the digger and she worked much better. I did not seem to get on very well today, got the rig done and set another so that I shall rig the wall side off. I started at the low end and made my rig up a fur. I brought my bicycle over today and got it cleaned this dinner-time, and it does shine. Fine day.

June 3rd Tuesday

Up a few minutes after five, got the horses and, after breakfast, I went to plough. I got the rigging-up piece done, but no more. I had to go to the station for some packages for Tomlinson. One was a hamper full of flower pots, weighing a bit over a quarter of a ton, it was very warm coming up the hill. William and the boy are busy clipping sheep, as most of them are around here. I have been reckoning up what I have spent up to now and such like tonight as I came in from *taking the horses, and I found a few mistakes, but I have put them right and have got it to come to just as much as I have left, which I could not before. Been a fine day.*

June 4th Wednesday
Did not get up till half past five so was thrown a bit late. Got the horses and cleaned them, then I went to plough. I had a few gays to run off on the throwing out piece. Got them done by dinner and then took the fur up and set another rig. I clipped a sheep at dinner-time, I also did one yesterday. They have got the lot done now. I took the horses and got washed. When I got back, the midges were awful keen down in the slack. Our cornfields are yellow over with brassocks now, especially the howe field, the big field has a lot in, too. Most people's are, about here. Very hot day, it looks almost like coming some rain tonight.

June 5th Thursday
Got up at five and went for the horses. Got them all right and, after breakfast, I went to plough. I had a rig to set and got almost done by dinner-time, as I am rather hurrying on or I shall not get it done this week. It came on wet after dinner when I had got back to the field, but I was able to lie behind the wall and so did not get very wet. It faired up a bit, but kept coming on showers all day. Our Hannah has been over here today. Very wet at night, I had to hurry to get up the hill from taking the horses out. I came up the street in Ben Simpson's carriage.

June 6th Friday
Got up at five, went for the horses and brushed them, then went to plough. I had a rigging up piece to do, and got it done by dinner. After dinner, I had the throwing-out piece to do, but it came on a nasty shower and I had to shelter for a half hour or so, and I did not get the fur taken up as I had hoped. I have been looking over my bike lamp and cleaning out the bad carbide, for I shall be going to Pickering tomorrow if it is a fine day. They have got a start to play at quoits at Levisham now on a night, it seems to go better than cricket, as it does not want so many players. Not a very fine day.

June 7th Saturday
Got up at five, went for the horses and, after breakfast, I went to plough. I had a fur to take up and a rig to set. I set it six yards from the wall, as it is only a small piece but too big to make into one throwing-out bit. I got the rig done by dinner-time. After dinner, I took the fur up, then set the headlands rig and then ploughed them. I have finished ploughing the field, I have been five and a half days over it. I got ready and went to Pickering at night on the bike. Had to pedal all the way as the wind was facing me. Got home all right, about eleven, was at Pollie Milestone's. Hannah was over today.

June 8th Sunday
I did not get up before eight or nine. Tried my new shoes on, kept them on all morning because it was wet and I did not go out. We did not go to the band room. We all got ready after dinner, when it faired up a bit, and went over to Pollie's. Stayed a while, then Pollie, Mannie and the children all went to Cropton Wesleyan chapel anniversary. There was plenty of room, but it was not a good entertainment. Hannah and Frances stayed all night, but Tom and I came home. We left milking till morning as it was nearly twelve when we landed. Very wet morning, fine night.

June 9th Monday

Got up a bit before five. Tom was up before me and had milked the cows by I got up. I had a bit of breakfast, then went to Levisham. I had to change my clothes when I got there, as I had left my working clothes there on Saturday night. I went to harrow in the boak field with the chisel harrows, but only used two of them, three would have been too much for two horses. It took me till night to get it done. I brought my bike to Milestone's on Saturday night and put her in one of the outhouses. I brought her over this morning, she is not very dirty as the road was dry. Been a cold day.

June 10th Tuesday

I did not wake up till half past five, so had to look a bit sharp. I went for the horses. After breakfast, I took all three and went to drag. I did not get it done till night, as the drag only takes a small breed. It is Lockton tea feast and I never knew till after I had got the horses turned out at night, or I would have let the boy do it, and have gone, but it is too late now. All the other boys out of the village have gone. Our people are busy stooking corn. Mr Robinson was setting a gatepost in the boak end field and I had to give him a hand with it this afternoon. Been a very windy, cold day.

June 11th Wednesday

Got up a few minutes past five, went for the horses and, after breakfast, I went to the five acre field and started to harrow. I was using the chisel tooth harrows, but only used two, as they were plenty for the horses, and we used the straight harrow boak and thought it might break if we put the three harrows on. I got it done a bit before night, so went and yoked up into the big chisel harrow and harrowed the headlands wall, then did a bit up the big field wall side, as there are a few wicks there, but not a very big breed. Our Hannah has been over today. I have taken the horses into the church field tonight. Cold, windy day, wet at night.

June 12th Thursday

Got up at five and went for the horses. I was able to get back a bit sooner, seeing I had them in the church field. I went to do a bit of harrowing. Used the big chisel harrow first thing, then the straight tooth set. Got about half way across, then yoked to the chain harrows and harrowed the wicks up the wall side till dinner. It is a bit clotty for the chain harrow to do much good, so, after dinner, I started to roll it. I did not get it quite all done, but not far off. At night, we had a good play at quoits - had two games and won them both. William and the boy have been scruffling. Been a fine day.

June 13th Friday

We did not get up till quarter past five, but got the horses into the stable by six. Went to finish off rolling, got it done by nine, then yoked up to the straight tooth harrows. I did not get it all done by dinner-time, so had to come back to it after dinner. Finished it off about four, then I turned one of the horses loose, old Diamond, and put the others into the chain harrow and started to chain harrow over against the big field. I only got a bit done before night. When I tried to catch old Diamond, she galloped round the field three or four times and, when I caught her, I gave her a few thrashes, and broke the blinder rein with the job. Fine day, was hot.

June 14th Saturday

Up at five, went for the horses, then, after breakfast, I went to chain harrow. William and the boy came to gather the wicks off and burn them. I was all morning before I got it done. In the afternoon we started to lead manure onto it. Got a breadth done down by the big field wall side, then it was night. I took the boy the cows out, and he took my horses out, as it was handy for me seeing the cows go into the seven acre on the boak. I took a cow belonging to Frank Pickering on with me, as she had got strayed, and, when I met Frank, he offered to give me 2d, which I did not accept. Pollie and Mannie came tonight. Been a very fine day.

June 15th Sunday

Did not get up very soon, about six, as I was up late last night. Washed my feet before the others got up, then helped to milk, got breakfast, had a shave, then a play on the cornet. Mannie and Tom and I set off with the children. Hannah and Pollie followed a bit after, as Frances got her frock wet with scattering some tea on it. I did not get in for the afternoon service, but the chapel was full. Mannie sang a piece by himself during the service. We stayed with the children and the women came home. I got in at night [to chapel] and was awfully hot as it was crowded. Very fine and warm.

June 16th Monday

Got up about five, had a bit of breakfast, then went to Levisham. the boy had got the horses in and, after breakfast, we started to lead manure again, got enough done to make a rigging-up piece and so, after dinner, I went to plough. I did not get it quite done, but very nearly. As William was in Pickering, we did not get done this morning till half past twelve, and so got a bad start after dinner. It has been that hot today I have almost boiled, especially at the manure leading job. I had a pair of new brown shoes on yesterday for the first time, also a green felt hat. I got them at Pickering on Saturday. Very hot day.

June 17th Tuesday

Got up at five, felt a bit tired as I was out talking till about ten last night. We had some more manure leading to do this morning, as I had ploughed all the other lot in. When we got to the field with the wagon, I took the first horse and the boy led it, and we threw an open fur where I shall have the next rig and then the horse walked down it. We only manured one side at a time, and it was enough to throw nine or ten yards as we did not get enough manured for a rigging-up piece. We had to keep at it all day, got the throwing out out piece done, too. Looks like thunder tonight.

June 18th Wednesday

Got up at five, went for the horses. After breakfast, I went to plough. I finished off the first rig then set another, did not get it quite done before dinner. I went back after dinner and just got half a dozen or so times about when it started to thunder and lightening, so I thought I would loose out and come home, as I saw a shower coming over the back of Newton and I had only my smock with me. It only came half a dozen spots and I should have taken no harm if I had stayed, but thunderstorms are hard to gauge. I was hoeing turnips to make the afternoon up. Everyone seems to be hoeing turnips now. Very hot day.

June 19th Thursday

Up at five, went for the horses, then after breakfast, we started to lead manure, as it was a nice cool morning with plenty of breeze. We were rather hard run into dinner-time, as we always get three loads in half a day, which is about as much as we can do, as we have to loaden and scale it on by ourselves. We have been leading away from this end of the midding[?midden], backing the wagon cross over to Betty's[?] yard. Put the horses in the limekiln field for their dinners. I *thought that I would pull the load round with Diamond, whilst the boy got there with the other horses, but she stopped just when the wheels were in the gutter in the front of the midding , and we had a bit of bother to get the horses to pull. It was three o'clock as we went up the lane, so we had to work hard to make it up.*

June 20th Friday

Got up a few minutes past five. Went for the horses. Was leading manure again today. We have got it nearly all out now except for a bit in the far corner against George Stead's shed. Jane has been to see Dr Clayton, and Hannah has been over, churning. Our people (Keaths) have got a litter of pigs last night, eleven and all living. We had our supper in the room tonight, as they were using the kitchen table for butter making. The boy and I were by ourselves, so we did full justice to our scanty fare. Frank Stead went down with me to turn the horses out. Had a walk round by the mill. Fine day, nice and cool.

June 21st Saturday

Up at five, went for the horses. After breakfast, went to plough. I had a throwing out piece to do, got it done by dinner-time. Did a rigging-up piece before I left in the afternoon. I was going to Pickering to get a pair of light trousers, but it got too late. Old Willie Hart gave me a few Brussel sprouts to take home to plant. I got home about nine or so, and it would be about eleven when I went to bed. Metcalf and Jackson came and brought William's wool. They did not take it away but weighed it up, did not come till about seven or so. Been a hot day.

June 22nd Sunday

Got up about seven. Got the "Sunday Companion" and read the summer number complete story. Had breakfast, then milked old Black-nose for Tom. Mr Pashby came up for his milk and stopped talking till it was too late for me to go to the band room, but Tom went. Hannah went to Stape camp meeting and I stayed at home. I milked at night and Hannah separated when she got back. She came home for tea, but Tom stayed at Baker's for his. I was going over at night, but it came in like rain and so I stayed at home, as I only have my best suit here - the other is at Levisham and I do not want to waste it. I have a cold, too....it did not rain. Fine day.

June 23rd Monday

Got up about five, felt a bit tired, but had to shake it off. Got something to eat, then set off for Levisham. I took my cornet with me as I intend to have a practice. I went to plough. Did a throwing-out piece, then after dinner, set a rig and got it ploughed up before night. I told Tom to send a pair of light trousers up with William, and he sent me a pair. I left some money at home for them, and Tom was going to Pickering, so I thought he could get me a pair as good as I could myself. Johnny Welburn went down with me with the horses at night. Been a dull, cold day.

June 24th Tuesday

Did not get up till nearly half past five, went for the horses and, after breakfast, we had to lead a truck of coal for Tomlinson. Took the wagon and cart and, as we came back with the wagon load, old Diamond lost a shoe, so we could not bring her back. Sent the boy down with her and the wagon, and I went for a cart load with the other horse. It came on very wet and poured down, and I got my jacket wet through before I could get to the station. I went into Stead's buildings till it was fair. We have got four loads up today, it was a nasty afternoon for the job.

June 25th Wednesday

It was half past five before we got up this morning and so I hurried up a bit. We had a wagon load of wool to take down to the station, took all but Robinson's. We were told that it had to go into the warehouse but, when we got there, we had to wait till the train brought a truck for it, and it threw us late for dinner. We could only get one load this morning [of coal] and it was wet most of the time. Got the lot up this afternoon. Had a bit of bother with Jet in the wagon, but made her to pull at last when we got to the top of the first hill, but she would have her own way and nearly sent the wagon over the side. There was 5 ton 15 cwt of coal. Wet morning, fine afternoon.

June 26th Thursday

Got up a bit past five. Did not go for the horses as William said last night that I would have to help them to hoe the turnips, as they are getting very big. And they are, as I soon found out, and very rubbishy, too. We were hoeing about half way up, then we turned back, as the bottom end was where the biggest turnips were. We have got all that end hoed off. Some were done already, as William and the boy have been on for more than a week. At night the mill boy came up and was shouting among the other boys against our gate and annoyed Jane with his bad language. Been a nice cool day.

June 27th Friday

Did not get up till nearly half past five. Cleaned out the cow shed till the boy brought the cows, then helped to milk. Went to hoe after breakfast, the others came a little later. Hoeing all day. Did nineteen rows from the hedge side. Johnny Welburn was on tonight about it being a rum one that they had no lead player in Levisham and had to come to Stape for one. So I told him a few things straight, which shut him up. Our Hannah has been over here churning today. There is nothing at all going off in the village now, cricket and quoits seem all to have dropped through. Been a fine day, damp at morning. We have had some stinking meat for a day or two.

June 28th Saturday

Got up about five, helped to milk when the boy got the cows brought. We got the swedes hoed this morning, and started on the yellow one after dinner. They are great big plants, too big by half to hoe easily. I went to Pickering on the bike at night, as I wanted to change the trousers which Tom got for me last Monday, they were too big. I got a pair the right size, then went to Pollie Milestone's and had a bit of supper. It was late when I set off - about eleven - and I arrived home at twelve or half past. Came up by myself, there was not many people in Pickering tonight. We have taken the horses down to low Swallowdale for the weekend. Been a fine day.

June 29th Sunday

I did not get up till nearly nine, and no wonder, for I should not get to bed till half past one or two o'clock. We did not go to the band room, I had a practice on Tom's cornet at home. Hannah went over to Saintoft, then Pollie is going with her to Middleton. It was Newton Wesleyan anniversary today. I went up at night, but was a bit late and could not get inside, there was a nice lot of people there. I came back by Stony Moor at night with some other moor boys. Been a very fine, warm day.

June 30th Monday

Up about five, got ready and set off for Levisham. Brought my bike with me (I left her in one of the Milestone's out-houses on Sat. night). We have been hoeing turnips again today. I have had my new trousers on today and they seem very nice and cool. I had a good play on the cornet tonight in the barn, had no-one but myself. I got myself a new pair of shoes at Pickering on Saturday, but left them at Pollie Milestone's. I shall get them this week when our folks are down. They are for weekdays, but I may keep them for wet Sundays, for they have no hob nails in the soles. Been a nice cool day.

July 1st Thusday

I did not get up this morning till a quarter to six and I had a bad headache. The worst of it was, that I had to got to Swallowdale for the horses, for the boy and William are going to dip sheep. I have been ploughing. Got a throwing-out piece done this morning and set the last rig nine yards from the wall. This afternoon, got it ploughed up. The throwing out piece that is left is only about ten yards wide, so it will soon be over for that field now. Have taken the horses down to the church field, for they broke through the Swallowdale gate and got into the seeds last night. Fine, cold day.

July 2nd Wednesday

Got up about five or so, went for the horses. After breakfast, I went to plough, got the throwing-out piece done and the bottom headland before dinner. the top headland was very hard, so I had to use the plough, and she did seem a rotten thing to use to the digger. When I had done the headland, I did a bit of harrowing to make up the afternoon. At night, Frank Stead came to see if I would go to Newton tea feast, so I sent the horses out with the boy, and went. It was rather tame. Stape band was playing a bit. Fine day.

July 3rd Thursday

Got up at five, went for the horses. Had to go to lead coals, and we have a truck in today for ourselves. William helped us to loaden the wagon and cart. We had a "Jib" with the wagon load in the morning - we had Jet in the shafts and, against the first turn, she would do nought but back, and we all but got the wagon into the beck against Stead's buildings. William got a great big birch stick and gave her it a bit rough. We had to loose her out and Diamond to put into the shafts, then we got up all right. Got three loads up both morning and afternoon, making six for the day. We took a cart load up and put it in the wagon each time, so we had some good loads on. There is 5 ton 10cwt of coal. Been a fine day.

July 4th Friday

Got up a bit past five and went for the horses. After breakfast, we went for the few remains of the coals. We left the wagon at the hill-top and brought a cart load and put in her, then got the rest on the next load. I had a nasty job throwing the coals back from the coal hole to the far end, for the place is almost as full as it can be. In the afternoon, I went to harrow the five acre, got it done by night. We caught a hare against the boak gate, so we sent it home with Hannah, as she has been working here today. I got almost wet through during the morning. Wet, roakey morning, better afternoon.

July 5th Saturday

Up at five, went for the horses. After breakfaast, went to roll the five acre. Thomas Pierson came by with the horse so we tried Jet, but she said "no thank you". I did not get it all done before dinner. Finished off after dinner, then I put the roller in the corner against the gate, and started to harrow up the far side, as it was a bit rough and a few wicks, but it harrowed too much manure out, so I gave it up and chain harrowed it till night. Took the horses out and went home.

Hannah has gone to Middleton to help Mrs Brewer with the tea tomorrow, as they expect the Stape Wesleyan choir to go tomorrow and will have a lot of them for tea. Fine day.

July 6th Sunday

Up at seven or half past and helped Tom to milk and separate, as Hannah is away at Middleton helping the Brewers. Tom went to Middleton about dinner-time. He borrowed my bike to go on. The Stape choir are giving a service of song at Middleton chapel this afternoon. Some of them went in Tom Snowden's motor car. I had to milk and such like at night, so did not go anywhere. I have been having a right good read today, reading the stories in the Sunday Circle and in the Companion. Mother has been working about all day, but has gone to bed tonight not very well. I went to bed at nine or half past, good time for Sunday. Very wet morning, but fine afternoon.

July 7th Monday

Did not get up till about half past five. Went outside with the gun and got a rabbit, but it was an old doe with young. Went to Levisham. Was a bit late and they had got their breakfasts, so I did not bother to go in for any. I felt rather thin by dinner. I went to scruffle, but it was so very claggy and drove all the soil onto the top of the turnips, so I gave it up and we started to hoe turnips instead. Before we loosed the horses out we rowed up the potatoes, did not get them done so very bad seeing I am not used to the job. John Stead came to see if they could have the grass reaper tomorrow. I went over to Lockton at night, got some sweets from the shop. Been a damp, roakey day.

July 8th Tuesday

Got up at five and went for the horses. William asked me if I would help the boy to milk, as he was going to John Stead's to cut grass. After breakfast, we loaded the wagon with phosphates and took it up to the five acre on the boak, then I came back for the drill. Old John Stead was helping us, as William was helping them. It was a very nasty roakey day. We started to drill about a quarter past eight, and did not give over till we had got it done, and it was a quarter past two. We have drilled most of it with rape, except about an acre at the far side which we drilled with turnips. Drilled it up and down with two horses, got a very fair mark today. It is the finish up of turnip sowing. Been a damp, roakey day.

July 9th Wednesday

Got up at five, but had not to go for the horses as we took them down in low Swallowdale last night, and I am going to hoe turnips today. William had to set Welburn off with the reaper, but he got back about ten. We have got the bottom end of the turnips done up as far as Robinson's middle field of cow pasture. After dinner, we started to hoe the headlands. Began against the potatoes and went right round the field, as there are three rows of swedes left up the limekiln field fence side, and rubbishy beggars too. The turnips are almost smothered with brassocks, as we haven't got some of them scruffled yet, and they are very bad to hoe. Been a very fine day, hot in the morning.

July 10th Thursday

Got up at five and went for the horses as we want a scruffler horse, and the others wanted a drink. After breakfast, I took old, lame Jet and went to scruffle. Started up the fence side, my word, what a job it was! Had to stop about every ten yards and clean the rubbish off the knives. The one which Alf Leng made the other day blocks up the worst, it won't clean itself a bit. I could not get on very fast, but got the swedes done by night. We took the horses down in Swallowdale again tonight. William and the boy have been hoeing turnips against Robinson's cow pasture. Went to the reading room at night, there is nothing on here now at all. Fine day, like rain at night.

July 11th Friday

Got up at five, went for the horses from Swallowdale then, after breakfast, went to scruffle with lame Jet, and turned the others out into the limekiln field. Was scruffling all day. Do not seem to get much further as there is such a lot of rubbish that some of the rows you cannot tell where they are, as the brassocks are about 8" high all over and awfully tough, they do nothing but drive on the knife. I took the horses down in Swallowdale again tonight. At night, was down at the reading room and had a game of bagatelle, my partner and I won the first game but lost the next. Tom has been over tonight with my bike which he borrowed last Sunday. People are busy now with their hay. Been a very fine, warm day.

July 12th Saturday

Got up at five, went for the horses. After breakfast, I went to scruffle again. I took the big old drag-cum-scruffler and used it with the drag teeth in, as there was too much rubbish for the scruffler to cut through. Ben Simpson came and helped to hoe a few turnips during the morning. The brassocks were so rank in some places that I could not see the rows and had to guess, but got through them by night, then went a time or two about with the scruffler. I shall have all the rows to scruffle up that I have been using the drag teeth on, as it did not cut more than half the rubbish, because we can only get three teeth to go on, which could not do much. Hannah has been over, I went back with her. Fine day.

July 13th Sunday

Got up about seven and helped Tom to milk. Got breakfast, then sat down and had a good read till about dinner-time, when I washed and changed, then Hannah and I went to the Newton camp meeting. There was just a nice gathering. I went over to Pollie's for tea and found her with a bad headache. Pollie and Nora came to set me - we thought we could get a bit nearer by going through Saintoft yard, but it seemed to be further round than the other. Saintoft children were shouting and telling us the way till we got out of sight. I was too late to get to the chapel, but did not mind that too much. Been a warm, sultry day, like thunder.

July 14th Monday

Got up at five and mother made me some breakfast ready, then I set off for Levisham. I was in time for my breakfast this morning. William has been culling the Swallowdale seeds today and I have been scruffling again. Found an old hare in a trap which we have set on the potatoes to catch crows. William went with me to help take the horses out. George Stead wanted someone to go with him and Frank to take a cow to Robinson's bull, as he is a bit saucy, so I went. But he did not turn any of his awkwardness out, and it would have been worse for him if he had, for we were well armed with sticks and stones. He had gone for William on Saturday night, but William managed to get out of his way. Been like rain all day.

July 15th Tuesday

Up at five, went for the horses. After breakfast, I went to scruffle, finished them this morning, hoeing turnips during the afternoon. Took the horses down to Swallowdale at night. Our Hannah has been over today pulling berries and they have got about twelve stone off. William has taken them over to George

Metcalf with the trap tonight. It has been very much like rain today, but has not come any. Frank Stead was showing me a postcard he has got from Laura Aflerson today, he seems quite pleased about it.

July 16th Wednesday

I did not go for the horses at morning as we shall not want them today. We went to hoe turnips during the morning. They have got big and overgrown, full of brassocks. We went to Swallowdale after dinner to turn the seeds. We only got half of it, or a bit more, done. I helped to milk at night. We took the horses down to the beck down in the valley below Swallowdale for a drink, and brought the sheep back with us, as they have been on the moor a day or two. Our boy was very late back with the cows, we had our supper before he got home.Been a fine day.

July 17th Thursday

Got up at five and went for the horses. The boy took Diamond and old Jet and turned them out in the limekiln field. I took the other in the horse rake to Swallowdale. We turned her off whilst we got the rest of the hay turned, and it was dinner-time by then. After dinner, I was horse raking. I was riding, and the old rake took an awful lot of jacking up at times when she got full. Had to hold the lever all the time or she would have risen and run over the top of the hay. Got it raked by about half past three, then helped William to cock it, also helped after I got the horses turned out at night, for which Jane gave us some more supper about ten o'clock.

July 18th Friday

Got up at five, went to Swallowdale for the horses and, after breakfast, I went to cut grain in the cow pasture. William came about ten and said I had to help them cock hay, as it was looking like rain. But it did not come, we had it all up by dinner-time. After dinner, I got another start to cut grain, and we finished it before we left at night, but it was about seven or after. It has not cut up a very big crop, but very fair at Robinson's hedge side. We have brought the reaper home tonight to go to Ben Simpson's tomorrow. Rather dull morning, fine afternoon.

July 19th Saturday

Got up at five and went for the horses. After breakfast, we went to cut Ben Simpson his grain in the field at the side of the church. It is very   [?]   up the lane side and Jet would not have it, she kept stopping and running back, so, about ten or half past, William brought lame Jet, and then we got away without much bother. I came up and had my dinner, but William stayed and I brought his down for him. When we got done, we came home and cut the little field between the lanes. I brought the cows home for the boy, as I took the horses out before supper. Been a nice fine day.

July 20th Sunday

Got up about half past seven or so, but did not do any work. After breakfast, I had a good read. Washed and dressed about dinner-time, then Hannah, Tom and I went to the Dale Camp meeting. There was a nice gathering at the afternoon service and as many at night. Father did not get to the Camp meeting, but went to the Love Feast at night. Saw Mrs Thacker, but did not speak to her. Frances has been poorly today with a bad cold. Elsie and Annie Woodmancy came here for their teas. Nice, fine day.

July 21st Monday

Did not get up till half past five, then got myself ready and came to Levisham. Mother has not been very well this morning, so she could not get up. We started to lead hay this morning. I forked the first load and loaded the rest, but we only got on very slowly, as we could only run one wagon and it is a long way to Swallowdale, for we were loading from there. Got six loads all the day, and it would be after nine by we got done. I took the horses away, and it was half past nine when I got my supper. I have had toothache all day. Been a dull day, like rain.

July 22nd Tuesday
Got up at five, went for the horses, then we started to lead hay again. We were leading hay till dinner-time, but it came on that windy we were forced to give over, as it was blowing it all away. William and I went down to the churchyard and raked it up and cocked it, and it was night by we got it done, for it would be nearly 2 o'clock before we got our dinner. We took the horses down to the church field when we went down after dinner, and left them there. It has been a most awful cold day and kept coming roakey showers, which made things worse. We have a calf very poorly.

July 23rd Wednesday
Got up about five. It was a very nasty, roakey morning, so I thought I would not go for the horses. We were cleaning out the boxes and calf house during the morning, as it was too rough to work outside. In the afternoon, we limed the cow house out and such like jobs. I was down at the reading room at night, they had a fire in the far end and it was very cosy and warm. The other end is in readiness for the show. The old .....?...has been in all night. it does not seem much better weather yet, and a strong wind with it, too.

July 24th Thursday
Got up at the usual time. Did not go for the horses, as there was nothing they were wanted for. William has gone to the Yorkshire Show at York, so we are by ourselves. We went to mow thistles in the limekiln field at morning. I fed all up before I went. At afternoon, we were among the hay, turned the little field between the lanes. Then it was time for the boy to go for the cows, so we went and straightened up two rows of cocks in Swallowdale. Came home and helped to milk and feed all up. Been a dry day, but dull.

July 25th Friday
Got up about half past five and went for the horses, as I thought we might need them, but we all went to turn hay in the cow pasture. got most of it done before dinner, then helped till about four, when I started to horse rake. Raked the little field between the lanes, then came down to the cow pasture till night. I have been looking for a puncture in my bike's front tyre, but have not found it. Hannah has been over here today. It has been cold and roakey.

July 26th Saturday
Got up at five and went for the horses at Swallowdale. After breakfast, the boy and I went to lead hay out of the little field between the lanes. When he had fed the calves, William came to help us. I forked whilst the boy loaded. We got it all at two loads before dinner. At afternoon, we went to finish off leading the Swallowdale seeds. We got them all, but did not get them all unloaded, as we left two loaded wagons in the stackyard. We have got one stack up and have got a nice start on another. I did not go home, as it was late when we got done. Hannah has been over cleaning for the .....?.....Been a fine day, but slow haymaking.

July 27th Sunday
Got up about seven and went straight home and got breakfast. When I landed, our folks were uneasy because Tom had gone out last night and had not

got back, but he landed in all right. I did not go anywhere till night, when I went to Stape. It was preaching at the Wesleyan chapel, but they held it outside as they are busy renovating the chapel. The floor was all torn up in places. Tom went to Saintoft after dinner, he had not landed back by I went to bed (but I saw he had landed when I awoke next morning).Been a fine, hot day.

July 28th Monday

Got up at half past five, got a bit of breakfast, then went over to Levisham. I went to horse rake in the cow pasture, got it all raked up by dinner-time. I had Jet in the rake and she tried to turn some of her badness off, but I got a stake out of the hedge and tried my best to knock some of it out of her, she went better for it, too. We have been leading hay today, but only got one load as the other two had taken a lot of unloading. Got the stack done and left a load down in the stackyard, as we have a fresh bottom to make. We have two stacks made now. Hannah has been over today finishing off her cleaning job. Been a very fine, hot day.

July 29th Tuesday

Did not get finished last night till after nine, so felt a bit tired. We went down for the churchyard hay this morning first thing, there was a nice little wagon-load of it. Jet turned awkward in the church field as we were coming with the load. William gave her a proper good thrashing and we almost trotted up the hill, William was giving them it with a thick stick. Part of our load came off against Armstrong's garden. Got the cow pasture led this afternoon, left two loads on the wagons tonight. George and Thomas and Sara have come tonight.

July 30th Wednesday

Got up at the usual time, got the horses, then got ready and took the reaper to the boak end field and started to cut. Got the biggest part of it cut before dinner, then, when I got done, cut along the top behind the quarry. There was a lot of mole-hills on the top and down the roadside. Got it done as much as I could with the reaper, then went twice round the other field. They are rather awkward fields to cut. Have had Diamond and Jet and they have gone well. We got done a bit sooner tonight, and we want to sometimes, as we have worked till dark those other nights. Been a nice cool day.

July 31st Thursday

Got up a little after five and got the horses. We went to cut the grass on the hilltop at the bottom of the big field. Did not get it done till about half past four in the afternoon, as it is such a nasty piece to cut, especially just below the corn, but got it done without such a lot of bother. Brought the reaper home, then brushed the horses and took them out. Got ready and went with Frank Stead to a circus at Pickering. We went on our bikes, and we did go, too! The circus was pretty fair, went in at eight and came out at ten. We got home about eleven. There was a lot of people there. Been a fine day.

August 1st Friday

Got up at the usual time. Went for the horses. After breakfast, yoked up in the grass reaper and went to cut Ben Simpson his grass in the field over the beck on Lockton. It was a decent crop, but not heavy, as he has pastured over summer. I had Diamond and old Jet and they went without so much stopping, got it done by dinner-time, then brought the reaper home. It is the finish up of grass cutting for this season, as we finished ours yesterday. they have been busy tonight preparing for the show, our boy is showing some turnips, they are a good size, too. We have got all our hay raked up, and most of the boak end field cocked, so that we shall have to finish it off. Our folks have gone to Blakey. Hannah has been over today. Been a fine day.

August 2nd Saturday

Got up at half past five and went for the horses so I should have them handy to water at dinner-time, took them into the limekiln field till dinner. The boy and I have been cocking the rakings in Swallowdale cow pasture and in the little field, then we came and took the horses back again to Swallowdale. I had dinner, then went over home to get changed, as it is Levisham show today. Got back about three o'clock. There was some very good stock and some farm and garden produce. I got the first prize in the sports in the evening for the best trimmed lady's hat. There was a fight outside the pub at night between old Wise and another man. It has been a very hot day.

August 3rd Sunday

Did not get up very soon. Got my breakfast, then cleaned out the cows and helped to mlk. James Pashby came up for his milk and I was talking to him, for a long while, then I went over to the band room. We only had a poor practice as there was only a few there. Had my dinner, then washed and changed, as it is our evening meeting. Robert Smithers was our preacher, we had a nice company but not a lot. Tom went over with Mannie last night and landed about five at night. I did not go anywhere at night, Hannah went over to Saintoft, they intend going to Scarborough tomorrow all being well. Been very hot today.

August 4th Monday

Got up about six. I am going to stay at home today and help Tom among his hay. It was very windy first thing and so we could not get on as fast as we should have liked. We went to the high land for some bracken for the stack bottom. Got a start to lead about ten or so. James Pashby came and helped us a bit at night, so we got on a bit faster. Got a nice looking heap gathered together, but did not get the lot. Only left the high side of the third field and a bit at the low side, but he can get it tomorrow easily. Windy morning, calm afternoon.

August 5th Tuesday

Got up about five, got some breakfast, then went to Levisham. Had some breakfast, then unloaded two wagons of hay. I went to horse rake the boak end field, as they got it led yesterday. They'd had Rickenson to help them and he was here again today. Got the first field done, then went into the other. We had a bit of bother to get the rake through the middle gateway, but Rickenson lifted her through. I brought the rake home when I got the two fields done, and the others gathered the rakings out of both and also the little field, but did not get them unloaded. Nice fine day.

August 6th Wednesday

When we got up this morning all was rather wet, as it had come a shower during the night. I went to scruffle in the five acre and it went all right, as the only rubbish is a few brassocks. After dinner, we unloaded the hay. It came on a nasty shower and we had to shelter a while. When we got done, we went to Swallowdale for the seed rakings. There was nearly a load, so we brought them home, and went with the other wagon and got the cow pasture rakings. It is the finish up of the hay time for this year.

August 7th Thursday

Got up a bit past five, went for the horses, then I went to scruffle again in the five acre. Took young Jet and she went very well, but I could hardly see the rows when the sun was full on them, as there is such a lot of runch at yon side of the field. I have been scruffling all day. One of the scruffle knives broke this afternoon, so I brought it down and Thompson, from Lockton, welded a new blade on it, and made a tidy looking job of it - better than Alf Leng. I have had toothache bad this afternoon, but it is much better now. Harry Walker came for a sheep tonight. Been a nice cool day.

August 8th Friday

Got up usual time and went for the horses. After breakfast, I went to scruffle with the same horse I had yesterday. The scruffler knife went champion which was new yesterday. I got the rape done and a few rows of turnip at the far side before dinner. It came on a thunder shower at dinner-time so I did not get back much before three, but managed to make a finish by night. It was an awkward job seeing the rows in places. Our folks have been cleaning out the cistern[17] today. I was down when it started to rain and it did rush in while it lasted. Hannah has been over today. Fine day except for the thunderstorm at dinner-time.

August 9th Saturday

Got up at five, did not go for the horses as we don't need them. Last night, I took them down to the far ing, so I shall get off the watering job. Harold and I went to hoe the turnips in the five acre, we have about an acre or so to do down the big field side, we did not bother to single them off, just put our hoes through. It came on wet when we got back after dinner, so we went to the quarry and sheltered. It did not fair up much till night, so we left off hoeing. William has been at Scarborough with the choir trip. I have had toothache bad today. Fine morning, wet afternoon.

August 10th Sunday

I got some of mother's colic drops on my teeth last night and rubbed my face when I went to bed, and I have not been bothered with toothache today. I got changed after dinner and went over to Stape, as Mr Temple is holding an open-air meeting. Got there in time to hear him preach. they had the service in the chapel at night, and it was almost full. I came home for my tea, but Tom stayed for his at Bob Masterman's. It was Newton sports last night, and it has been all the talk today about the goings-on there was at night. Been a fine day.

August 11th Monday

Got up at half past five and mother got my breakfast ready, then I came to Levisham. it was about seven when I landed. the boy was just coming out of the gate with the cows, so I thought they had had their breakfast. I went and asked William what I had to do, which he told me, and I said I'd be going on, as he did not offer me any breakfast. But I met the boy coming back from taking the cows out, and he told me they had not got their breakfast yet, as Jane had not got up, but I managed till dinner. We have been hoeing turnips all day. William has not been with us, as he has been to Pickering. Been a fine day.

August 12th Tuesday

Got up about five but did not go for the horses, as we should not want them. Set some snares last night and I went round them, but there was nothing in. I helped to milk and then went to hoe turnips, or rather, seconding swedes. We started up the fence side, the swedes are yellow with brassocks, and the others are almost as bad, as anyone may know, it took us all morning to get a time about with two rows, and only cutting thistles and brassocks, at that. William and

I went to mow bracken on the common in the afternoon. The boy went to Pickering to the Ryedale show. I was out watching the fireworks at night. It has been a very fine day.

August 13th Wednesday

Got up about the usual time. Did not go round the snares, cleaned the stable out instead, there was two barrow loads of manure in it. When we got milked and done up, we went to hoe the swedes, but it came on wet about eleven, so we knocked off and came home and straightened the turnip shed. It faired up after dinner, so William and I went on the moor again to cut bracken, while the boy kept on with the turnips. We have got a nice patch mown, we shall be getting them home before we cut any more. I was at Lockton last night with Reg. Frank went with us. We were only there about a quarter of an hour. Reg wanted some shoes soling. I see they have got a cobbler together now in the old butcher's shop against the hut.

August 14th Thursday

Got up about five. When the cows were brought, helped to milk. After breakfast, Harold and I went to second the swedes again. William stayed at home and put the stone over the cistern with mortar, and he was pulling the haystacks and straightening them up fit for thatching. We went round the snares at night and put some longer pegs in to hold them higher. It has been Whitby horse show today. Robinsons have been with a pair but did not get anything. One of them here got the silver cup. Been a nice day.

August 15th Friday

Got up about the same time, but went for the horses this morning, as we want to take the young pigs away. Taylor, of Newton, bought them. We took them over the bridge going to Newton, then we let them out. Three of them ran back to the beck, and one of them fell in a deep place, but swam out. The railwaymen came and helped us. William came as far as the common, then he want back to heap bracken and got a small load. When I came back, I took out the horses before dinner. William and I have been thatching a haystack this afternoon. I thatched one side, it is the first time I have done any, did not get on so bad. Jane has been at Pickering. Hannah has been over today. Been a nice day.

August 16th Saturday

Got up about five. Did not go for the horses. When the cows came, helped to milk. There was a hare in the snare this morning, someone had been round before and got one out as the .....[?].....showed there had been something in. We started to thatch the other haystack this morning. We ran out of thatch about dinner-time, so, after dinner, we took the pony and trap and went to the station slack and cut about ten sheaves, for we only wanted enough to thatch about a yard on either side of the stack. We got it done with six sheaves, however. I came round home by the station. Tom has gone to stay all night at Saintoft. Been hot day.

August 17th Sunday

I did not get up till very late, in fact, it was nearly nine, but I slept badly so it was excusable. I did not do much of aught today. James Pashby was up at morning and I had a talk to him. I did not go anywhere at night, as there is nothing worthwhile walking over to Stape on a Sunday night to see. Tom came back about six, and we sat down to read till ten. Father was sat in the garden gathering up some seeds, as it was beginning to roak a bit and he *did not want them to get wet, and reaching down to pick them up, he fell on top of Hannah's dahlias and broke a great armful off. Of course, he was no worse.*

August 18th Monday

Got up about six. I am not going to work this morning, instead I am going to Whitby regatta. We set off from Levisham station at a quarter past eight, and set off back home at the same time pm at night. I was going about with Henry Holliday's son, George, out of the dale, and Arthur Magson, John Stead's "boy". We had a good look around, but I did not see much of the races as there was such a crowd watching. I lost my pals a bit after dinner, but found some more folks I knew so did not mind much. I brought a few pieces of seaweed for our boy to look at. It has been a beautiful day.

August 19th Tuesday

I got up about six. Mother asked me if I would stay at home and help Tom to lead turves[18], which I did. Tom went and got Fred Smith's wagon so that we could get on a bit faster than with the cart. We did not get a very good start and only got five loads, which is ten rooks. We are making a turf stack in front of the shop. The turves do not seem to be in bad form, but some are rather damp. Hannah went over to Pollie's to get some sewing done, so we were by ourselves. I came over to Levisham at night, as I thought it was the best way, then I shall not have to dash in the morning. It has been a fine day.

August 20th Wednesday

Got up about five and went for the horses. After breakfast, the boy, and I went with the cart for some sheaves they had cut yesterday down in the station slack. Brought them back, then went with the wagon for a load of bracken. William came with me. It was very shaky for the wagon on the common as there are so many big stones. We went down and got another wagon load after dinner. We are stacking them along the wall side from the zinc shed to the hen-house. I took the horses away at night down to the ing, and stopped at the hill-top among some other boys when I got back. It has been a fine day.

August 21st Thursday

Got up at the usual time and went for the horses. We went for some more bracken, took two wagons this morning, and brought the lot. We ...[?]..... them after dinner, then William sent the boy out with the horses , and we started to thatch the haystack. Did not get a start till almost three o'clock and got about half of it done. I have been learning to play a tin whistle I got at Whitby, I can knock a tune out of it now. It has started to rain tonight, but don't suppose it will be much. It comes in dark now about eight o'clock at night, so that we do a bit of reading. Been a very fine day, damp at night.

August 22nd Friday

It had been raining during the night, but faired up by we were got up and kept fine. Got up a bit past five, but did not go for the horses, as we shall not want them today. William and I pulled the binder out and started to clean her. We were rowing about her till about eleven, then we started to thatch the haystack where we left off yesterday. William was ill during the afternoon, so I had the haystack to finish off on both sides. We have got the haystacks thatched now. I have done the sides next to George Stead's, and William has done the others which catch the storm more. I had a good practice on the tin whistle till dark. It has come on a wet night.

August 23rd Saturday

Got up at half past five, it was a wet morning. I helped to milk, then went with the boy to mow bracken. We went to cut a patch which goes over to Bolton's. We were mowing bracken all day and it has been rather warm down there, we took a turnip down with us for lunch. William has been a little better today but has not done much. Mr and Mrs Coates came to spend the weekend with the Keaths. There was a lot of good bracken that we were mowing and it was hard work. We had some fried meat at dinner-time which was set fit for a dog it was so old. It has been a fine day, after a wet start.

August 24th Sunday

I sat up reading till the small hours of the morning and, in consequence, I had a splitting headache when I got up this morning, if I could call it that, for it was half past nine. Winnie Milestone came this morning for the day, she will be going back tomorrow. Tom and I went over to Stape chapel at night, we got inside too. It was the Wesleyan, and it is the first Sunday since its renovation. I thought it looked very nice, but not very fancy. We came home with Baker and Pierson, got home a bit past nine. It has been a showery day.

August 25th Monday

Got up about five and mother got me some breakfast ready. I came to Levisham, brought my mouth organ this week and left my tin whistle at home. I did not get any more breakfast. The boy and I were sent to set some wire nets along George Stead's hedge joining our Swallowdale, as William wants the lambs on the fog soon, and the fence is a very bad one. After dinner, we were mowing thistles in the other side, we only got about half of them done. We had our supper by ourselves, William and Jane got theirs before, and we had such a laughing going-on as never was about a cat that I threw at the boy. It has been a fine day.

August 26th Tuesday

Got up a bit past five and helped to milk, when the cows were brought. After breakfast, I went with William to get the sheep which were on the common against the boak gate. Some of John Stead's were among them. so we had to sort them out. William and the boy were among the sheep most of the morning, they are speaning the lambs. I have been down among the bracken all day. William with the boy joined me about eleven and we had our dinners on the moor. Robinsons, George Stead and Banks haave got a start at harvesting, started on Monday. It has been a very hot day.

August 27th Wednesday

Did not get up till half past five this morning. Went for the horses and, after breakfast, went to lead bracken, took both wagons. Harold was loading the first lot and, when he was about three parts loaded, we pulled the wagon out a bit and it went over a small bump, which brought the boy off, and the bracken, as well. After that, I had to loaden. It's a very bad place to get a wagon out of. We nearly had the wagon over one time when the hind wheel went into a hole and she was standing on three, but we got her pulled out all right. We have got four good wagon loads today, but only got two unloaded, the other two are on the wagons. We shall have to start afresh and stack. It has been hotter today than yesterday.

August 28th Thursday

Got up about five and went for the horses. After breakfast, we unloaded the bracken, got the stack finished off with the first load. We have got the space from the red hut to the shed filled up with bracken. We put one of the loads in front of the boil house and made Jane a chicken house in one end of it. Then we went to the moor for the rest of the bracken. Got it in one load and was home before dinner. In the afternoon, we unloaded the bracken, then Harold took the horses away, and we were fettling the binder the rest of the day. It has been a fine day.

August 29th Friday

Got up at five, but did not go for the horses. I helped to milk. After breakfast, William and I ground the old scythe, then went to open the corn. We started in the big field and got round it by dinner-time, I was mowing most of the time. After dinner, we went to open out the howe field, and it took us all the afternoon, as it was a good crop round the headlands. I was mowing, the boy gathered and William tied. At night, I helped to milk. It has looked like rain this afternoon - it did thunder and come a very light shower. Hannah has been over today. It has been warm.

August 30th Saturday

Got up at five, did not go for the horses, but helped to milk. After breakfast, William and I went down to the church field to milk some of the ewes, as we have them down there since the lambs were took from them. I brought the horses back with me and geared them ready for the binder, then we took the binder to the big field. Got about half a dozen times round when one of the cobble trees broke, but it was dinner-time, so did not bother us much. Got one off the old drill, which just fitted. After dinner, I rode one of the pole horses and drove old Jet in front. A rotten job, too, we have about half of it down. It has been very hot today. Stayed all night .

August 31st Sunday

Got up about seven. Went with the boy for the cows, then I came home. Got my breakfast when I landed. I have had the toothache very bad this forenoon. Pollie Milestone came up after dinner and Winnie went back with her at night. We had a look up on the moor, but it was too bad weather to go far. I have not been anywhere at all today. Tom went over to Saintoft at night and has not come back - he will be staying the night. It has been a nasty, roakey day, and is still keeping at it. I went to bed anout half past nine. It is father's birthday today, he is 76 years of age. Tom did not come back.

September 1st Monday

Mother called me about five and told me it was a worse morning than ever , so I thought it was no use going to Levisham, as we could not harvest. I helped to milk, then got ready and went to Pickering. I got the tooth pulled out which had been aching so, and another old, decayed one as well. Place pulled them out. I bought a pair of gloves for loading corn with, as I don't know if our folks in Levisham will have a pair or not. I also put a small sum in Barclays bank. My teeth did not hurt so very much, but plenty.

September 2nd Tuesday

Got up a bit past five. my face ached a bit, so thought that I'd stay at home today, as I might get cold in them if I went to Levisham. I helped to milk and separate, then was shaping besoms for Tom, we got about eight dozen made, then ran out of laps. I came over to Levisham at night, as it is best to come over the night before, then there is no hurrying off in the morning. Our people did not say anything about me not coming over before, but they knew as I saw William at Pickering on Monday. Cold damp morning, fine afternoon.

September 3rd Wednesday

Got up a bit past five, then went for the horses and brushed and geared them, then we went to cut corn. They had been cutting a bit yesterday afternoon, and we finished it off before dinner and came into the howe field, but did not get a start before dinner. It came on a roke when we were going back, so we sheeted her down and went to stook some of the oats we cut this morning. Some of it had been done and we finished it off about five or so. William and I then went to open the bull field out, it is barley. We got very wet with stooking, as the sheaves were dripping wet with the heavy roke. Fine morning, roakey afternoon, till it faired up about four, but came on again at darkening.

September 4th Thursday

Got up about five, went for the horses and brushed them ready for work, but it came on a roke so we turned them into the limekiln field and went to open out the barley. It was fine weather by ten, so we came and got the horses and went to cut the oats in the howe field. We got seven or eight times round, then loosed out for dinner. We went back after dinner and got on well till about four, when it came on rainy, and we were forced to loose out. The boy went for the cows, while William and I put on some old bags and stayed and stooked all that was cut. Got very wet with the sheaves, but it did not rain so bad, came on roakey. Roakey day, fine from 10 to 4.

September 5th Friday

Got up at twenty past five and went for the horses. After breakfast, we went to cut corn. It came on roakey just before we got it done, but we did not stop and it faired up by eleven. We shifted into the bull field, just got her set down, then we came for our dinner. We have to open half of it out yet, so we went up after dinner and opened it out. Came on wet again about three or four, so we had our lunch till it faired up. William and I came and finished stooking the howe field, and Harold went for the cows. got it done a bit after six. The horses are staying in the limekiln field tonight.

September 6th Saturday

Got up a little past five and went for the horses. After breakfast, went to the bull field to cut the barley. It is a very good crop, there are a few thistles over the top end where the potatoes were last year. William had a knife to sharpen, it was too blunt, it would not cut. The horses went fairly well this morning, it has been a better day, should get round about fourteen or fifteen times before dinner. The binder did not go over well and we had a nice few stops, but got it all down, though it was late by we finished, as the old binder kept going wrong. I am staying here the night, as it was nine or so when we got done. We have got all cut. The horses became tired before we finished. It has been a fine day.

September 7th Sunday

Got up about seven and went to look for my jacket which I had laid in the bull field somewhere, but could not find it anywhere. Came home round by the common. Got some breakfast, then sat down to read till about dinner-time, when I got dressed up and went to Nathan's meeting. Dixon was preaching, did not reckon much to his talk. When I got home, I went to look for the cows but did not find them. I came over to the church [at Levisham] at night, and stayed here. Tom went for a walk with Pashby this afternoon, I met him coming back as I went to Levisham. I had to rush to get to church, but got there in time. Went for a walk with Magson after church.

September 8th Monday

Got up about five, went for the horses and, after breakfast, turned them into the limekiln field, as we did not need them. William brought the sheep in off the moor as they will get rong[?] and we side longed some of the ring leaders and milked some which had a lot of milk in their bags. When he got the sheep into the limekiln field, we went to stook the bull field. William went to Pickering in the afternoon, and the boy and I finished stooking, then came and started to mow the tares, we did not get them all done, but nearly so. William did not find the cows till almost dark. It has been a fine day.

September 9th Tuesday

Did not get up till six this morning as we were working late last night and were tired. I went for the horses and, after breakfast, went to the station for some coals. Armstrongs have a 8ton 16cwt truck of coals in, and we shall have them to lead, and in the middle of the harvest! We got a few in the wagon and brought to the hill-top, then brought a cart-load and put into it and went back for another cart-load, which we brought home. When we got our dinners and the coals unloaded, we went to lead corn out of the bottom end of the big field where there was a lot of thistles, made almost two little [...aykes?]. Got three loads, and it was late by we got done. The last load was an awful looking beggar, it pigged [?] off at the binder end before we got it loaden, the boy loaded with a fork.

September 10th Wednesday

Got up a bit sooner than yesterday and went for the horses. We put them in the boak end field last night, as there is more meat there for them, and it is handier for us on a night. We emptied the wagons then went for some more corn. William went to the station to throw the coals out of the truck. We got two loads before dinner, have got a start to make a long stack. We got three bits of loads yesterday and have nearly got all the field cleared. It was dark by we got the last load tonight and the moon did not shine, as it was inclined to rain, but it was not much.

September 11th Thursday

Did not get up till about six, then went for the horses. We had two wagons to unload first thing, then went for some more corn, got two loads before dinner which cleared the big field. After dinner, we went to lead the howe field oats. Got one stack made out of the big field oats and stacked the howe field corn in front of the cow house. Got four load in the afternoon and unloaded three of them. I unloaded all but two load today. It was nice and moonlit tonight, we should be working till nine, bit past nine when we got our suppers, but we took the horses out before. It has been a fine day.

September 12th Friday

It was half past five when we got up this morning. I went for the horses and, after breakfast, the wagon load of corn had to be unloaded, then went for some more. Got one load, when Ben Simpson came to help us. We cleared the howe field with two loads this morning and also got two out of the barley field before dinner. We got the thistley ones in the afternoon, the top first, and William made them into a round stack down in the stackyard, but the others he put up against the granary steps at the end of the oat stack, leaving a road for the cows between. I have been loading today. There was a lot of thistle. Old Ben forked pretty fast but our fork people at home got on rather slow, I got down home with the wagon almost every time. It has been a fine day but very much like rain.

September 13th Saturday

Got up at half past five, went for the horses and, after breakfast, we unloaded both wagons which we had left loaded last night. When we had got that done, we started to lead some more. It had been a sup of rain last night, but it got blown off by the time we started to lead. We got three load before dinner, but were late in, as it would be one o'clock. We got two load afterwards and cleared the field. It is the finish up of leading sheaves but, of course, all is to rake yet, but there won't be many rakings. We unloaded the wagons before we milked. There was just enough to top the stack out. I took the horses down to the ing for over Sunday. Stayed all night. It has been a fine day, like rain tonight.

September 14th Sunday

Did not get up till half past seven. It was rather a wet morning, but faired up about eight and never rained anymore during the day. I came home, got breakfast, then read a bit. Went over to the band room but nobody turned up. It was our meeting. I stayed till Tom went out with Pashby for a walk round by Keldy. Mr Welburn was our preacher, he did not stay for his tea, but he talked very well. I am going over to Stape tonight. .....I went, but was too late for the chapel.. I walked to Newton with Arthur Nicholes and Bob Shaw, but there was very slow doing there, almost as bad as Stape. It has been a windy day, drying up nicely.

September 15th Monday

Got up a few minutes past five and mother made me some breakfast ready, and I came to Levisham. Got some more breakfast when I landed. Afterwards, took the horse rake and started raking the bull field. the boy has been using George Stead's [rake] in the big field, William borrowed her this morning. After dinner, I went to rake with George Stead's rake in order to ease the boy a bit, as it is a tiring job walking all the time, did not get it all done but nearly. Jane has been at Pickering with the marketing. She is groaning with a bad hand and the doctor told her that she has got rheumatics in it. It has been a fine day.

September 16th Tuesday

Got up at half past five, went for the horses, then I took our horse-rake and went and finished off raking the big field. It took me till dinner-time to finish it off. George Steads wanted their rake back this morning, but lent her to John Stead, instead. I shifted our rake into the howe field and went a time or two round before dinner. In the afternoon, we all three went to clean rakings up. Went and cleaned the bull field up first. The boy loaded and got such a queer load I thought it would have come off, but we tied it down at twice before he got it loaded, then had to prop it tied after it got home. We went and cleaned the rakings out of the big field afterwards. It has been a fine day.

September 17th Wednesday

Got up at half past five and went for the horses. After breakfast, I went to rake the howe field. It was a cold morning and came on a right storm just before I got it done. I was almost frozen riding. I only had the leather reins with me or I would have walked. Brought the rake home with me and had dinner. After dinner it was still raining, so we went for the binder between showers and for the rest of the afternoon we were pulling implements in the low shed, cleaning the binder and such like. Very cold and wet.

September 18th Thursday

Got up about the usual time and went for the horses. After breakfast, went to lead a few more of Mr Armstrong's coals. Took the wagon and cart. We brought *up a few in the wagon, then brought a good cart-load and emptied it into the wagon and went back for another cart-load. It was late dinner-time by we got back. William had gone to help Robinson to thrash this afternoon, and it was rather late by we got the wagon emptied, so we only went for one cart-load after dinner. Did not take the wagon (William told us to do so). Our Hannah is over today baking for Miss Keath, she is staying all night. Our housekeeper has a strange groaning sat with her hand.[?] It has been a fine day.*

September 19th Friday
Got up at half past five and went for the horses. After breakfast, we went to the station for some more coal. We only brought two load up this morning, one in the wagon and the other in the cart. The horses have gone extremely well leading from the station this time. We emptied the cart before dinner. William had to go to help the Robinsons to thrash this afternoon. We brought the remainder of the coals up in the cart after dinner, and, when we had got them emptied, we went and cleaned the rakings up in the howe field. Helped to milk the cows, it was late by we got done tonight. It has been a fine day.

September 20th Saturday
Got up about half past five. I went for the horses, as we expected all of us being at home today, but Robinson's boy came while we were at our breakfast and wanted a hand to go to thrash, so I had to go. We were thrashing in the middle yard, I was jacking straw with George Hammond. We only had six yards to carry it, but a nice bit up a ladder, as old Willie always gets them a great height. After dinner, John Steads were thrashing and we all three went. I was among the straw again with three others, as we had it a long way to carry down the stackyard, they did shove it through! I am not going home tonight. It has been a fine day.

September 21st Sunday
Got up about half past seven and it was a rather damp morning. I went home and helped mother to milk - mother seems to do all the milking now, as she is a bit better than she has been of a long time. Jennie and Mary Hannah and baby were down for the weekend and also two of the Brewer's boys, Duke and Harold, came, so we had plenty of noise and not much comfort. I went to Milestone's meeting and some of the Pickering's boys were there. The preacher could not start the tunes very well, Mrs Bolton's sister started one time. I had a good laugh at Stephen Eddon - he went for a pot to give some girls a drink and fell and broke it. It has been a fine day, damp morning.

September 22nd Monday
Up at half past five, got a bit of breakfast, then set off to Levisham. Went to John Stead's to thrash, I was among the straw again. Welburn and I were kept going carrying it right through into the barn. When a few more came, I went into the rully and forked it through the window. I was doing this till the barn was full, then I carried straw again down the stackyard. After dinner, we were thrashing in the stackyard, we finished about five. I was among the straw, we had to go between two stacks and it was a bit tight. Jane has had some people here sleeping for the weekend called Schofield. It has been a fine day,

September 23rd Tuesday
Got up at half past five, went for the horses and, when I got there, there were no halters, the boy had brought them home when he took the horses out on Saturday. So I drove them down, they did come! We started to lead manure into the little field between the lanes. We manured the top half joining Morley lane,

and William is going to spread phosphates on the other half to see how it grows. Got done in good time at night and went down to the reading room, have got the fires in now for the first time today. It has been a nasty damp day, kept coming on a nasty shower, neither wet nor fine, but enough to make work a misery.

September 24th Wednesday

I did not wake up this morning till a few minutes past six when I heard William going past the door, so hurried up as we expected going to Welburns to thrash, but they were not on. I should think they want the stack tops to dry up a bit. We were cleaning up the yard during the morning, also siding up the barn and the granary fit for thrashing, but, after dinner, William went to the Stape church opening and Harold and I went down the garden and started taking up potatoes. They were a heavy crop, got about two bags full. I went for the two cows we keep in the field, Harold went on the moors for the others. it has been a very fine day.

September 25th Thursday

Got up about half past five and helped to milk when the cows came. After breakfast, I went to Welburn's to thrash. I was among the straw. I forked into the barn, but the sheaf hole was right behind the stack that we were thrashing, so that we could not get a wagon in, so I made a big heap of straw to stand on so that I had not so high to fork it. I was kept going and it was a hot job. I had the engine and thrasher to shift at night and the engine started to leak in the fire box and spouted out right over the fire box. Thomas Robinson said it was our fault for shaking her. It has been a very fine day.

September 26th Friday

Got up about half past five and saw that the engine was still running, it is a bolt head that is burnt almost off. I went for the horses and we took some stakes in the cart to Swallowdale to stop up the hedges, as William wants to turn the old ewes in when he gets the lambs turned into the rape. We were doing this all morning. After dinner, we went to take up potatoes in the field, I ploughed them up and Harold led the horse. They were a very good crop, but we only had six rows, got them all taken up and took home. We put them in the calf house against the wash house. The crows had got about half of them when they were newly set. It was a damp morning but a very fine afternoon.

September 27th Saturday

Did not get up till almost six. William said I was to bring a horse in, as he did not think the engine would go to enable him to thrash, but, when I got back with the horse, Thomas Robinson had got the fire lit and Isaac Sedman was filling her with water. She did not lick much after the fire got a start, we did not get a start till nearly eight o'clock. I was forking straw through the sheaf into the barn out of the wagon. It was oat straw and very heavy, I had a warm job. After dinner, we thrashed the barley and got it through by half past four, then had to side up. It has been a very fine day. I stayed all night.

September 28th Sunday

Got up about seven. Got an old bass which was in the stable and went out mushrooming to bring home. I did not find many in our fields, as someone else had been before me. I lit on James Pashby gathering mushrooms in our howe pasture at the boak end, but there was none there, so we came down to George Stead's intakes and found plenty, we got our basses full and had mushrooms for our dinner. I did not go far today, went nowhere in the morning, but at night

I intended going to Stape or Levisham, but instead went nowhere. I sat reading a good bit. I did not get to sleep very soon as Harold Brewer kicked about so.

September 29th Monday

Got up about half past five and mother made me some breakfast ready, then I set off to Levisham. George Stead's were thrashing this morning and William and I went I was forking off the stack and it was not half a bad job, neither. We only had a short half day, as we did not start much before half past seven or eight and had done by eleven, we had an excellent allowance. In the afternoon, Harold and I were drawing barley straw for thatching, William went to Pickering. The old engine fire bars dropped down into the fire box this morning, she is about done. Thomas let all the water out of her when she had got done thrashing. It has been a very fine day.

September 30th Tuesday

Got up at six or thereabout. I thought we, perhaps, should not need the horses, so did not go for them. After breakfast, started to draw straw for thatch out of the barley stack. It was not a very nice job as there were a lot of thistles in it, Harold and I were drawing most of the morning. After dinner, I started to thatch. Started on the long oat stack and did the north side first. It was rather windy and made it bad to do as the straw was very light, I put some water on it to make it lie. I got my side done by night. William has been thatching the little....[?]...... at the end against the shed. Hammonds have been shifting the engine and thrasher today. Been a fine day but windy.

October 1st Wednesday

Got up about six or so. I thought that Hammonds would be on thrashing, but saw that the engine was not lit and I was told afterwards that they cannot set her on till some new fire bars come, as the others are done. I started to thatch the south side of the long stack, but ran short of prods, so I started on a round one on the other side. Harold and William went for some prod sticks and just landed about when I had got the last of the others used, so I was not stopped. Got the round stack done at morning, and got the long one done all but fastening down the last course. It has been a fine day.

October 2nd Thursday

Got up at six and went and tied down the thatch which I did not get done last night. After breakfast, I started on the round barley stack, but ran out of straw, and so came and drew a bit till the boy came, when he drew and I got a start thatching. It took me till six or half past to get it done. It was Lockton harvest thanksgiving tonight, I went over but was too late for the service. I was with Frank Stead. As we went, we found a piece of rotten wood up Lockton hill which showed a bright glow, we were puzzled to make out what it was. It has been a damp day.

October 3rd Friday

Got up at six. Went for old Diamond as the man who brings the dip cart wanted a pull-up from the mill. I got my breakfast and went down, he had got there when I landed. We set down in John Stead's yard and I helped to dip. I was at the tub holding their fore-legs, one had got hold of their heads, and another hold of their hind-legs. We got through by dinner-time. Our's, Hammond's and John Stead's are the only three that dip that way. I helped him back to Lockton and, while I was there, got old Diamond shod all round new shoes. It has been a fine day.

October 4th Saturday

Got up at six and went for the horses as I thought they would be thirsty, which they were. It came on to rain before I landed down with them and rained till dinner-time, it didn't half rain! We were flaying oats all morning and barley during the afternoon. Our Hannah came over here this morning and got wet through. I went home with her at night and it was fair all the way. Manny and Polly and two girls have been to Whitby today and they said it rained every bit of the day.

October 5th Sunday

I sat up reading till two o'clock last night, or rather, this morning, so did not get up very soon, it would be about seven or half past. It was raining and pouring down and continued so till about dinner-time, when it started to fair up a bit and got out fine about three or four o'clock. Manny started up in a great rush, he would go home. So there was a packing up and a general fuss and chuntering, but got them ready, and set off about four. Hannah and Frances and I went to set them and we nearly went to Saintoft. It got out a grand night. Mother seems to have got a nice lot better and can now get out and milk regularly, I am very glad she can. Very wet morning, fine night.

October 6th Monday

Mother called me about half past five and I got a bit of breakfast and came to Levisham. I am coming over in my strong boots today as you need something to stand on, as wet as it is now. I started to thatch one of the stacks - it is the last one to thatch - and got half of it or more done by dinner, but would have got it all done if I had not run out of stick prods. William and the boy were limbing an old sycamore tree down on the garden and I got some prods out of it. I got the stack finished about three and then went to help Harold, who was taking potatoes up in the garden. Jane and William have gone to Pickering. It has been very windy. It was very awkward thatching on account of the wind.

October 7th Tuesday

I did not wake up this morning till I heard William coming down and it was half past six. I went for the horses and, after breakfast, we started to lead manure onto the tare stubble and the potato land. We had the two Jets in the wagon, left Diamond as she has to go to the station at dinner-time with the Tomlinson's luggage. We got three loads of manure from home, then started leading from the manure heap just through the gate in the limekiln field (we led it there at Spring for the potatoes). It came on wet about four o'clock and poured down, I got wet through. Changed into my breeches and leggings. We are sleeping the horses in for the first time, as it is too wet to turn them out. Hannah was over and had to stay all night. Fine morning, wet night.

October 8th Wednesday

Got up at six and it came on thundering and raining a few minutes after. I had the horses to clean and such like and, after breakfast, I went to finish off leading manure, gave it a good thickness. After dinner, I got ready for the plough and went and made a start. I set a rig right up the middle of it as there is only about 25 yards or so. I did not get very much done as the plough was to be put together. She had her wheels off. I had a bit of bother to get her set right. We are sleeping the horses in again tonight and don't expect they will sleep out anymore this year. I have some more coke to lead for Armstrongs tomorrow, all being well. Rather showery.

October 9th Thursday

Got up at six, cleaned the horses out and fed them, then got ready to go to the station to lead a truck of coke for Armstrong's. Got two loads both morning and afternoon. took the wagon and the cart. The horses have pulled well today, never once offered to turn awkward, but then we could not get heavy loads on as it is that small coke that old Ned used to call breezes. We had to take it through against the postman's hut, and tipped it just behind the greenhouse wall. William and Ben Simpson have been pointing the house roof as it rains in all over. William has given us the stable lamp tonight. We had to use the old lantern before, and it casts a much better light does the lamp. It has been a fine day with only one or two showers.

October 10th Friday

Got up at six and cleaned the horses out. After breakfast, we had some barley to bag and took five quarters down with us, our's and Welburn's are going in the same truck. We only got one load of coke up at morning and one after dinner, as we had the barley to bag up and loaden and it took up a lot of time. William had the coke to shovel out, as the truck had to go out. Miss Keath has been to Dr Clayton today. Hannah has been over today. We got done in decent time, so loaded the wagon ready for morning. I went down to the reading room at night. It has been a fine day.

October 11th Saturday

Got up at six and cleaned the horses out, then got ready and went to the station. We took the cart with us this morning, as we shall be able to get two loads of coke up, seeing the wagon was loadened fit for going. We have got all fifteen quarters of our corn down now, altogether three tons. We had two little loads of coke left for the afternoon and have now got it all up. It was a fine night and I came round home by the station, as Hannah has been to Pickering and I helped her with her parcels. We had a gossip with old Mrs Fox when we got to Raindale. it has been a very fine day.

October 12th Sunday

I sat up till twelve or so last night and so did not get up till nine. Did not do anything, sat reading most of the morning. I intended going over to Saintoft but never got off. It was a lovely day and I could sit out on the grass and read. I have not been anywhere at all today except going for the cows at night, they have got into the bottom mill dam. Also had a walk round the fields before dinner. Mother seems to keep well, she gets about wonderful now with a stick. She does all the milking and gets the cows and lots more jobs. She looks much better since she got a start to get about again. It is the finest Sunday I have known in October, not a breath of wind.

October 13th Monday

Got up a bit past five. I did not feel very well, had a nasty headache and felt sick, but thought I'd go to Levisham, so set off. Felt worse when I got down the hill, so turned back. I was poorly most of the day. Tom went to Malton fair and Hannah went to work at Levisham. Mother and father took four rows of potatoes up - Tom ploughed them up before he set off. I cut some sods to cover them. I have not done much today. Tom came back with the last train. I sat up rather late. Hannah stayed all night at Levisham, it is their chapel harvest festival tonight. It has been a fine day, dull at morning.

October 14th Tuesday

I did not waken up till half past seven, mother said she thought she would not waken me. I was cleaning up most of the day as it has been very wet during the morning. I shovelled up the manure heap behind the cow house and cut a gutter along the barn side of the midden to let the swig run away. After dinner, I cleaned the mud out of the yard and swilled it, then got ready for the harvest festival. Tom has been helping to decorate this afternoon. I went at night, got in nicely before time. It was packed for all it was a very wet night, but it was fair weather when we left.

October 15th Wednesday

Got up about half past five, got some breakfast, then set off for Levisham. I was sent to plough. I got the bit in the pond field done and the plough shifted into the big field. After dinner, I went and set a rig along Robinson's wall side. Our folks have been thrashing at Hammond's today, they harvested a ton and a half of oats yesterday and brought the fire bars with them. I left ploughing in good time, as William and Harold were thrashing, and got the cows in and helped to milk. Has been a fine day.

October 16th Thursday

Got up about six, cleaned out the horses and such like. After breakfast, I went to plough. William and the boy have been sowing phosphate onto the little field between the lanes. It is some we had spare from turnip time, and William wants to see if it is good for the grass, as we manured half the field before. They are going to sow some on the seven-acre. This afternoon I have got the piece rigged up, but it took me till dark. It is Lockton Church harvest festival tonight, I was going then didn't. I went out at night to the reading room but they hadn't a light, so had a walk round by the back lane. It has been a very fine day.

October 17th Friday

Got up about six, cleaned the horses out and brushed them over. Harold and I went to Bank's to thrash. I was among the straw. We thrashed a small stack of oats and a big stack of barley. The barley was very dusty as it had been very much heated. We only had a light force at the straw, so they sent for William. There was only half a day's thrashing, I was ploughing during the afternoon, had a rig to set first thing. Ernest Welburn, Billy Meyers, Francis Stead and Jacky Ben were round tonight begging for the tar barrel, but they won't get one, only a few fireworks. It has been a fine day.

October 18th Saturday

It was a very misty morning. Got up about six and cleaned out the stable and such like jobs which have to be done among horses. After breakfast, I went to plough and have been ploughing all day. At night, I went into Pickering on the bike, arrived there about eight. I got myself a pair of new boots for Sundays for this winter, got them from Sawdon's. I also had my photograph taken at Smith's, at

John Brough, dressed in his best suit and posing for the photographer. (see October 18th)

the old coffee shop. Was at Pollie Milestone's, then went to our Pollie's at Saintoft for the night. They were in bed when I got there as it was about twelve. It was a lovely moonlight night, the bike went first rate. Got out a lovely afternoon, quite warm and summery.

October 19th Sunday

Got up out of my "shacking bed" about eight and sat around till ten, when I thought I would like to see a farm at Marishes station which was partly burned down during the week. There was a lot of people going on their bikes to see it, but it was only like an old barn without a top and a bedroom was burned. The roads were so dry and it was such a lovely day that I thought I would ride as far as Malton, went as far as the common and back. I came a very great speed back, on average a mile in five minutes, got back to Saintoft about two o'clock. After dinner Mannie and I went to see Keldy, they have got a lot of the roof on now.

October 20th Monday

It was a dark night last night or I should have come home, but stayed all night at Saintoft. I was going to have to come over to Levisham early this morning, but it is such a long way I thought it would be late before I could get there, so I stayed all morning and set off about two in the afternoon. Pollie has been making me some new shirts. I came home by Stony Moor, rode the bike almost right from Rawcliffe to Stony Moor hill top gate, got home by three. Our folks have been taking up potatoes. I did not do anything after I landed except help to milk. It has been such a fine day, came on like rain at night.

October 21st Tuesday

Got up at half past five, had some breakfast, then came over to Levisham. I came in my old Sunday suit and left the other at home, had to change when I got here. We have been leading coals today for the Rickenson's and the school-mistress, four and a half tons altogether. We had to weigh Rickenson's in a scuttle and it was a dodgy job. We nearly got them all up, I think that the few that are left will come up in the cart. It was dark before we got them all out, we left half the coals in the wagon. I did not go to the reading room, I have been busy in the stable writing up my diary from Saturday till now. It has been a fine day, but rather dull.

October 22nd Wednesday

Got up at six, did the horses then, after breakfast, Harold and I went to the station for the remainder of the coal. We left the wagon at the hill top and brought a small cart load and emptied into her, then got the lot on the cart the next time. All the coals we got today are for the school mistress. I have been ploughing this afternoon, got the throwing out piece done but had not time to set another rig. People are busy around here sowing wheat, we expect our seed wheat coming sometime soon, I wish it would come while it is fine weather to get it sown. It has been a fine day.

October 23rd Thursday

I did not wake up till half past six so I was awfully late. I got the stables cleaned out and such like before breakfast and. while we were at our breakfast, Robinsons sent word that they wanted two of us to go and thrash, so Harold and I had to go. I was jacking straw all day. We have been thrashing down in the low yard. and we did not get done till about a quarter past six when it was almost dark. I went down to the station to see if Hannah had been to Pickering and brought my strong boots which are getting mended, but she had not been down,We were thrashing barley most of the day, then did a round pyke of oats which was the biggest part thistle. It did not get all put through as it was so late the old engine would shake the fire out after we shifted her. It has been a rather damp day.

October 24th Friday

Got up about six and cleaned out the stable. After breakfast, William and I set off for Newton Dale quarry for some stones for Ben Simpson. he is going to build Armstrongs a summer-house. Got two loads during the morning with one wagon, so we had no time to loose. We also got two after dinner, but took both wagons. Brought them loadened down the common both at once, old Diamond brought one. Then we took them up the hill to our five-acre gate, but, of course, only one wagon at a time. It was about dark by we got them unloaded. It has been a fine day but rather sharp air, been a keen white frost last night.

October 25th Saturday

Got up at the usual time and did my work in the stable. Ate breakfast, then Harold and I set off again to the quarry. William was with me all day yesterday, but we only have two loads left, so Harold went this morning. We got both loads home with one wagon before dinner, but were rather late as we had to sort some stones out to make up the last load. In the afternoon, I went to plough and had a rig to set up first thing. William and the boy have been putting a little door in the barn wall to let light in to the oil engine. They have made a very botchy job of it, too. I did not come home as it was too dark. It has been a lovely day, the sun felt quite hot.

October 26th Sunday

Got up at seven, I was among the horses till breakfast. I stayed for my breakfast for the first time for months. I took the horses out then came home. It was our meeting and we had Mr Brewer as the preacher, he stayed for tea. It came on wet after tea. Tom and I set off to see Legs who is very seriously ill, not expected to get better. We went by Baker's and it was raining fast, so we called in to shelter. Stayed there about two hours, then set off to Keysbeck Lodge as it had faired up a bit. We were not allowed to see him. They wanted someone to stay all night, so Bob Shaw and I stayed, we were in the kitchen and Legs was in the room. Very misty morning, wet night.

October 27th Monday

I came away from Eddon's a bit after five, Bob left half an hour before me. It was a fine morning and was almost broad daylight by I got home. Mother was just coming out when I landed and I said "good morning", and she was quite surprised that it was me, as she did not know that I had been out. I got changed then came to Levisham, arrived about half past seven. I went to plough and have been ploughing all day. I felt awfully sleepy in the afternoon with sitting up last night. Went down to the reading room at night. Been a fine day except a nasty shower at darkening.

October 28th Tuesday

Got up at six, did my usual work and, after breakfast, I went to plough. I was ploughing all morning. After dinner, we went to sow wheat. William sowed it broadcast and I harrowed it. Did not work very well, was rather claggy and wet. I harrowed it twice over lengthway and once cross-over. It was all turning doing it cross-over. William has about a bushel of wheat spare, I don't know what he will do with it as he has had it steeped in .[?]...t stuff. I did not do anything else *but harrow the wheat and so we got done in good time. I was over at Lockton at night. Old Walt went with me. Been a very fine day.*

October 29th Wednesday
Got up at six and did the horses. After breakfast, I went to plough and was ploughing all day. Harold had to go to the station at dinnertime with Tomlinson's luggage, they are going away today for good. I went over to Lockton to hear Miss Harland preach tonight, she is holding a fortnight's mission and she talked very well. William has had the copper on as he is starting to feed the pig. He used the wash-house copper as he thought the sparks from the boil-house copper might set the straw stack on fire. Been a fine day.

October 30th Thursday
Got up at six, cleaned the stable out and such like till breakfast, then I went to plough. I had a fur to take up and a rig to set first thing. Set the rig almost opposite the gate into the limekiln field. I have been ploughing all day. Went round the walls looking for a sock and found one much better than the one I am using, so put it on [the plough]. I went down to the reading room at night. Harold has been starting a dess of hay in the end stack for the horses, the first start of the hay this season, it turned out very good. It has been a very fine day, quite warm and sunny.

October 31st Friday
Got up at six then did the usual work till breakfast, then I went to plough and have been ploughing all day. Got the rigging-up piece done and a start on the throwing-out piece. I do not think there is much of aught to write about, except it keeps lovely weather for the time of year, there are lots of leaves on the trees yet and it is warm and sunny, you could almost fancy it was the first part of Sesptember instead of the last of October. Hannah has been over today, churning and baking for Miss Keath. It has been a lovely day. It is a fine night.

November 1st Saturday
Got up at six, it was a rather dark morning as it was foggy, so we had to have a candle to get up with for the first time this autumn. I went to plough after breakfast and have been ploughing all day. William went out mushrooming first thing this morning for the Hartlepools were expected today, but a letter came saying they would not come, so Miss Keath was rather vexed. William and the boy have been making some new legs for the old pulper, the old ones have rotted off. I did not go home tonight, Walt Farrow came and we stopped talking in the stable most of the night. It has been a very fine day.

November 2nd Sunday
Got up at seven and cleaned out the horses. After breakfast, I took the horses out, then came home. I brought Harold's rabbits over with me, as I am going to let Nora and Gladys have them, for the boy wanted rid of them for they were in the way. I went down to Milestone's meeting and Tom went to Saintoft, but I did not send the rabbits with him, am leaving them here for a bit for Frances to look after. I have put them in the old ferret box. I did not go anywhere at night. I set old Annie Cook home from the meeting, did not much care for the job as she is too wizened looking for me. It has been a very fine day.

November 3rd Monday
Got up about six or so, got some breakfast, then set off to Levisham. I was not asked if I had had a mouth when I got there, so went out to plough and have been ploughing all day. William went to the market. He has found me a new sock and

so I took it up after dinner and put it on and it made her go much better. I had a fur to take up and a rig to set first thing this morning. I am going on nicely with it now, a few more days and it will be ploughed. I stayed in the stable at night and wrote some letters with my fountain pen. I did not get any written as old Walt came, which stopped me. Been very windy and cold, but fine.

November 4th Tuesday

Got up at six, foddered the horses till breakfast, then went to plough and have been ploughing all day. Miss Keath was peeping about when I came in at dinner-time and she noticed that a bit of hair had got rubbed off Diamond with the trace, so I had to take some cloth up with me after dinner and have them lapped. I was going to do so myself without her mentioning it. I got the rigging-up bit done and a time or two round the throwing out piece before dinner. I am going to write tonight. I got my letter written. it was rather misty first thing, then got out quite warm.

November 5th Wednesday

Got up very late indeed - it was almost a quarter to seven - so had to look sharp. I went to plough after breakfast and was ploughing till dinner-time, then Robinsons brought word that a truck of slag had come in for them road and we have to lead it. We got a start on it after dinner. Got three cart loads, tipped two load in the Braygate hill opposite the quarry, the last load we brought as far as our limekiln field gate. The boys of the village have been having a few fireworks tonight, but such dozey ones I never saw the like, I would not have given them aught. Rather dull, got out fine.

November 6th Thursday

I almost felt ashamed of myself this morning as it was as late as yesterday when I got up, and we have to go to the station. We got two loads, one in the hill and brought the other into Morley lane. After dinner, led other three. Two of them we put against the gate at the top of the hill, but on the common side, and the other further down the road. Our Hannah has been over today, churning and baking. I saw several daisies and such like flowers out in bloom, also there are a nice few mushrooms yet, but are going back now as it is getting too late for them. It has been a fine day.

November 7th Friday

I thought I'd be up a bit sooner and woke just after five, so kept awake till about half past then got up. We went again to the station for the remaining stone. Brought a small load to the hill top against the gate and brought the rest almost to our limekiln field gate. We did a bit of rutting just out of the station gate as we had too many on the last load. There has been 9 ton 2 cwt altogether. we got them at ten load, but the first load we got and the one we got this morning would both have gone into one. I went to plough after dinner. Set a rig against the wall as I thought it might be misty in the morning. Did not get the fur taken up. Was misty at morning but got out fine.

November 8th Saturday

Got up at six, did the horses and, after breakfast, went to plough. Took the fur up first thing, then went to the rig. I have been ploughing all day, nearly got the rig done. I did not come home at night. Walt Farrow came down and we were putting a new ring into his watch, then we went down to the reading room. I think there is nothing worth putting down today. William and the boy have been boiling the copper today for over Sunday. William sold his lambs to old

Robinson of Newton on Wednesday, he has kept ten or eleven, I think. I saw some segrams out in flower today, also a great burr thistle down in the stackyard. It has been a fine day.

November 9th Sunday

Got up at seven, cleaned out the stable and such like till breakfast. Afterwards I took the horses out into the limekiln field, then came home. I did not go anywhere till night, when Tom and I set off for Newton to hear Miss Harland preach. She is over there now for a fortnight, the same woman as was at Lockton. We were too late for the service, so went over to Saintoft. I got Mannie to cut my hair as it was awfully long. We came back by Newton, and came round home by the station with Matt. He had had too much beer and was talking all sorts of religious subjects as we came down. It is a grand moonlit night. It has been a lovely day.

November 10th Monday

Got up about six, it was rather roakey and I was in two minds whether to come or not, then I thought the boy would want to go to Pickering, as it is the hirings, so I came. I went to plough but it came on wet, so I was forced to loose out and come home about ten. It kept on wet till dinner, then faired up and stayed fine, but was very foggy. William went to Pickering on the one o'clock train and did not get back till five. The boy went on the ten and came back on the last train. I have been whitening the cow-house out this afternoon and had to start in good time to fodder out, milk and such like. The cows go out at days yet.

November 11th Tuesday

Got up at six, did my work in the stable till breakfast, then went to plough. I got the rig done and a start to the throw-out before dinner. I have been ploughing all day. William and the boy have been having the oil engine on this afternoon pulping turnips and chopping. They have put a shelf on the pulper so that she will go with the engine, then they are going to give the cows pulped turnip and chop. It has been very misty today and cold, but kept fine till night, when it has come on wet. Harold did not get anything to eat from breakfast till he landed back at night [yesterday]. I think he was a fool to do so.

November 12th Wednesday

It was almost half past six when we got up this morning. After breakfast, I went to plough, got the throwing out piece done by dinner-time. After dinner, I started on the bottom headland. I rigged it up, got it done by night. It is dark now by five o'clock. It was a fine morning, but rather showery by afternoon. I went down to the mill with Walt Farrow at night to get his washing, but Arthur had brought it up. It is not such fine weather now as what we have been having, the mushrooms are all about done, but I saw a man gathering some in George Stead's intacks today, but it is not much warmer down there.

November 13th Thursday

Did not get up again till half past six, then did the horses and, after breakfast, I went to plough, had the top headland to do. I have thrown it out as I thought it would be best that way. Got it done by dinner-time without hurrying. After dinner, I was leading manure with the cart into the limekiln field. Started to put it across the top end as William said it would go up best now while the ground is dry. Got three loads but it was almost dark by I got it in at night. Harold has been setting some snares to try to get some rabbits for William to take to Hartlepool. Tom came over and had a band practice, the first. Cold, showery day.

November 14th Friday

Got up about six, did the horses. After breakfast, we started to lead manure with the wagon. I got one load up and spread on before Harold came to help me. First he had the cows to take out and his snares to see to, but he has not caught anything. Got three load before dinner and three after. William went away to Hartlepool on the three train for the weeekend, so we shall be with ourselves. Have almost got the manure out now, shall get the rest out tomorrow. Hannah has been over today. It has been a bit finer today.

November 15th Saturday

Got up about six. I did the horses and Harold did the cows, same as he always does on a morning. He also made the fire after breakfast. I yoked up and got a load of manure up to the field and Harold came and helped me to unload it. Got two loads out, then we loosed out as we had got all but the shovellings up. I shovelled it up into the wagon while Harold took the thatch off a corn pyke we want in. After dinner, we had the wagon to take away and it was rather blacky stuff to fork out. We had to look awfully sharp to get the stack in, got some queer loads and threw them into the barn chamber all ends up as it came on like rain. It has been a very fine day.

November 16th Sunday

Got up at seven. I did the horses then helped the boy to milk. After breakfast, I took the horses out to the limekiln field and came back and took the calves up to the bull field. Harold asked me to stay all day today, so I am going to. I went with Harold round the snares and there was a rabbit in. When we came home, I went into the house and read the news to Miss Keath. After dinner, I went down in the coke hole under the church with Jack, Tom and party and, my word, we did enjoy ourselves, I was laughing all the time. I went for the horses before tea, they had been right on the edge of the quarry and George Stead had to set them off. I went to church at night. It was a fine day, wet at night.

November 17th Monday

Got up about six. I did the horses and Harold lit the fire and did the milking. I went to plough and Harold had to do all up, the cows to take out, and the calves and such like. I had to go for my plough into the limekiln field and brought her round into the Swallowdale seeds. I set my rig up George Stead's howmer side but did not get much done before dinner. Miss Keath did not want to go to Pickering with the butter so Harold had to go. I was ploughing during the afternoon. Harold had seen some soldiers at Pickering and he is considering whether to join the army or stay in farming. Our Hannah has been over today. It has been a fine day.

November 18th Tuesday

Got up about six and it was a real wet morning and rained till after breakfast. I pulled the horses out but took them in again as it was like being a wet day. I went into the granary and was flaying a few oats over, which had dossed out when we were getting the stack in on Saturday. When Harold got done up, we went to pull some turnips and were pulling them till dinner-time, it was a nasty job as it was wet most of the time. After dinner, I went to plough and the boy went for the turnips. It rained fast as I went up the lane and I sheltered in the quarry. So did Willie Hart and he said some fond things about Miss Keath. William has got back. We had a kipper each for supper. Very wet morning, fine afternoon.

November 19th Wednesday

Got up about six, did the horses and, after breakfast, I went to plough. Have got the rigging-up piece done and a good start on the throwing-out piece. After dinner, word was brought that a truck of coals had come in for Arthur Hammond which we have to lead, so had to start on that. William went down and loaded the cart and part of the wagon, so that we got on a bit faster. We had them to unload and carry in, with scuttles at that, and it was hard on me when I came up and quite dark. Harold and I had a couple of kippers each to our suppers tonight. It's marvellous, Jane and William only had one each! William has brought a great parcel of kippers back with him, it will be kipper supper now for a fortnight! it has been a fine day.

November 20th Thursday

Got up at six and did the horses and, after breakfast, (I thought we were never going to get it this morning, Jane lay in bed late, Harold did not make the fire and William did not get up till seven) we went to the station for some coals. Got two loads and had to take them for Mr Harland, but they emptied them while we were at our dinner. They weighed them as he wanted two tons. We had a cargo of hay to get in at dinner-time. After dinner, we got the lot up, but there was two good loads, as many as three horses could pull. Only emptied the cart, but Harland and them emptied the wagon. It's kippers again for supper. I got a letter from Esther Booth. Our Tom came over at night and we had a band practice. It has been showery.

November 21st Friday

Got up at six and did the horses. After breakfast, I went to plough. Had some gays to run off first thing, which was about nine, and then the fur to take up, and also got a fresh rig set before dinner. My watch is at Pickering and I have to guess the time, have knocked it fairly well up to now. I have been ploughing all day, it does not slipe so well now as it did at the other rig. Harold has caught a hare and three rabbits by now, he also ran over one of Miss Keath's pullets with the wheelbarrow and killed it. Today we had two kippers again, William and Jane only had one and are prodding on with them for all evers. Hannah has gone to wait on a woman at Farwath so Willy has had to churn and make the butter up. It was showery am, fine pm. We feel strong on kippers!

November 22nd Saturday

Got up at six and did the horses. After breakfast, I went to plough and have been ploughing most of the day. Thomas Keath and Georgie and his mother came here today, but went away to Pickering at night. Georgie has been running about with a turnip lantern made into an old man's face which I made last night. At dinner-time William set the oil-engine off and cut some chop for the horses , as he will give the cows most of the chaff that is spare. The oil engine did not go very well at all, but we managed to get through what we wanted, also cut up an oil tin, how it got in nobody knows. It has been a very fine day. I am not going home tonight.

November 23rd Sunday

Got up at half past seven, did the horses and, after breakfast, I bedded them up, as it had been a hard frost and we thought they would be better in. I came home and went with Tom for a band practice, but it was poor as there was only a few there. Pollie and Mannie came over in the afternoon and went back before dark, I set them over and stayed all night. They had brought the old carriage over to the Stony Moor hill-top and we had an awful job getting it back on the highroad, we had a light or we could not have got on very well. We had the children to carry most of the way. Very dull and cold.

November 24th Monday

Got up about nine. Did not sleep very well on the shacking bed. I had a light and read a story part of the night. Came home, got ready and went to Pickering on the one o'clock train. There was an awful lot of people knocking about Pickering and four organs going making a lot of noise. The popular airs were "Who were you with last night?" and "Down in my home in Dixey". I was in a show where there were three sheep, one had three legs and the other two each had six legs, a big rat and bug, and also a two headed baby. I was in a picture show. It has been a very fine day. Harold has left.

November 25th Tuesday

I did not get up till late so stayed at home today. I am not going to have a Martinmas week as I can get a day off anytime. Tom and I got a stack in during the afternoon. Mr Pashby came for his milk and had a good long talk. Tom went out at night and did not come back before I went to bed. I think most of the servants would leave yesterday, very few left on Saturday. Mother gets about wonderful and does all the foddering among the cows and milks all by herself and does a tremendous lot of work now, but her leg gives her a lot of pain at times yet and is much swollen. It has been dull but fine.

November 26th Wednesday

Got up at seven, had breakfast, then came over to Levisham. I was rather late but they did not say anything. I went to plough and have been ploughing all day. Reg Masterman came over at dinner-time and wanted me to got over with him to Kit Morley's of Thornton. They are having a birthday party for one of the daughters. I got a very pressing invitation on Monday to go, but could not get off very well seeing I only came here this morning, felt disappointed all the same. We were pulping some turnips at dinner-time, also cut some more chop. The oil engine went a little better, but wants a lot of her own way. It has been a fine day, but cold.

November 28th Thursday

Got up very late - it was seven- as I have not got my watch yet and I am a bit puzzled to know what time it is on a morning. I did not get my watch on Monday. It was a wet morning so I did not have to go out with the horses. I started to work at the cistern. First I turned all the spouts off, which was an awkward job, then I had to pump the water out. There was not such a great lot in as she leaks, which is why we are going to mend her. We scraped all the cement away at the sides where we thought the water was likely to get through - it is an awful bad lining - then we filled the places up with fresh cement. We were at it all day. Tom came over and had a band practice. Dull, damp day, fine night.

November 29th Friday

Got up sooner this morning, did the horses, then helped William to milk. After breakfast, I went to plough. It is not a very nice job guessing the time by the sun, but I got in just as the others were coming, so I was all right. I went to plough after dinner and had a rig to set first thing. No, I had a fur to take up and then set the rig, have been ploughing all day. William has been churning today and he also had to turn the butter-worker, as Hannah is at Farwath and cannot get. She came up when William and Jane had got it made up and so she went. Fine day.

November 29th Saturday

Got up about six, did the horses and helped William to milk. Then I went to plough and I think I was ploughing all day, but have almost forgotten, as I never set anything down from now till December 10th, and so it takes a lot of thinking to bring to mind what I was busy with. William has been boiling the copper today. I am staying here all night. I was down at the reading room at night, but there is very thin deed. It is Malton Martinmas Saturday, I saw a few going this morning. It has been a fine day.

November 30th Sunday

I did not get up till almost eight, did a bit at the horses, then helped to milk and finished them off after. Went home but was too late to get to the bandroom. I read a bit till about three o'clock, then got changed and set off to Thornton. Went round by Farwath and across by the Fox, saw Hannah at Farwath. The chapel had started when I got down, Miss Harland was preaching. After service, I let on a certain young lady whom I had come on purpose to see, and I went home with her and her brother. I had supper and we sat up all night. Been a fine day.

December 1st Monday

I set off home about five. They were all in bed at Farwath, and at the other houses I passed they were just getting up, but landed home without anyone seeing me. It would be about half past six or seven when I got home. Mother was up and I did not want her to know that I had been out all night, so I waited a few minutes till she went to the front door to throw some water out, then I rushed in and stood in the shadow of the stairs, I had taken my shoes off in the kitchen so made no noise, then made it appear as if I had been in bed all night. I got into bed, as it was rather late to go to Levisham, and I slept till eleven, didn't I want it. Been a fine day.

December 2nd Tuesday

I got up rather late but went over to Levisham. It was about eight but I got some breakfast, then I went to plough. I believe I was ploughing all day. I had a fur to take up and set a rig just before dark. In fact, it was dark, and I could not see the rig sticks, so got rather a poor mark, but, however, got twice round it then left. I expect William will be wanting the rape land ploughing now before I plough any more seeds, as it is rather soon. I was down at the reading room at night and saw Robinson's fresh thirdy and the fresh bullockey. Been a fine day.

December 3rd Wednesday

I did not get up very soon as I am bothered to know the time when I have no watch, and it is a cold job getting up and coming down to look at the kitchen clock each time I awake during the night. I did the horses and helped William to milk, then I went to start on the five acre on the boak I am going to use the old plough as she is there in the field. I did not get much done at morning, was a long time making a headland mark round the field and setting my rig, but still, I got a nice start. I was ploughing all day, at least from about half past nine till half past four, and it is dark by then, so I don't have a very long day. It has been a fine day.

December 4th Thursday

Got up at half past six, did the horses, then helped William to milk. After breakfast, I went to plough and have been ploughing all day. I got the piece rigged up and also another rig set. I saw Isaac Sedman coming past so asked him if he had got my trousers made yet. He said they had been ready for weeks, so I shall have to go over for them some night soon. It has been a very cold day and I think we shall have some snow before long. Tom came over at night and we had a right good practice. Very cold.

December 5th Friday

Got up at the usual time and found it was snowing, though it had not got much down and faired up by breakfast. I did the horses and helped to milk, then went to plough as it is only about an inch deep and much warmer than it was yesterday. Miss Keath has been to Pickering today to see Dr Clayton. She looked for our Hannah coming over, but she is at Newton now, I expect, so could not get off. It has started to freeze and is freezing awful and keen. The road is very slape and the horses can hardly hold their feet where there has been a bit of traffic. I shall not be able to go to plough tomorrow if it keeps on.

December 6th Saturday

When we got up this morning all was frozen hard, so hard that I saw afterwards that the children could slide on the pond, of course, not right across the middle. I never saw it freeze so keen in one night. I helped to do all up, then went and took the ewes some hay down in Swallowdale. When I came back, I went to pull turnips as they pull nice and clean. After dinner, I went and brought some home, got two loads, but some of them were what William had already pulled. Afterwards, I got some hay in and such like. Tom came over and we had a practice, but only a poor one as it was club night, and William did not get to help. It has been a fine day but it is freezing again.

December 7th Sunday

Got up about eight, started on the horses and helped to milk then, after breakfast, finished off the horses and came home, did not land till about eleven. It was our meeting, so I had to help mother to get the house ready. We had an awful bustle on, as Hannah is still away, and the clock had been stopped, and the people began to come before we got the kitchen sided up. I rushed upstairs and had not got washed , so did not come down, and it was not very warm, either. Worst of all, the preacher, Mr Dixon, stayed for his tea and never went out, so that I was a prisoner upstairs. I was over at Stape tonight, was in the chapel. Hannah came a bit tonight, but had to go back. She is at Newton now,at Hardcastle's. Mr Welburn was preaching at Stape. Been a fine day, like a thaw tonight.

December 8th Monday

I got up in good time. Mother called me, she never knew but what I had been in bed all night, last Sunday night. I got ready to go to Levisham but waited a little bit till it got a little lighter, as it was a very dark morning, very thick and foggy. I got to Levisham just as William was getting up. I got my breakfast, then went to plough as the frost has nearly gone now. William went to Pickering at dinner-time. It is the Christmas fatstock show. I have been ploughing all day. Arthur Magson came up at night. He wants to sell his gramophone so he brought her up and we had her on in the stable. I bought her. Had her on in the house as well, only about ten tunes, but a lot more to come yet. It has been a fine day.

December 9th Tuesday

It was very late when I got up this morning, as I was on with the gramophone till ten, and it was seven when I rolled out, so had a bit of a rush on. William always gets up after me, about seven on average. The children had gone to school by I went to plough, so had a short half-day. I have been ploughing only half a

*day as William wanted some turnips pulping and some chop cutting. By the time
we got that lot done it was time to go for the cows - they go out yet on fine days.
I was siding up the stackyard at night for about half an hour. I was down at the
reading room at night, they have got two fires on now, not before time. Fine day
but dull.*

December 10th Wednesday

*I woke up this morning and it was almost light, so I jumped out of bed, I felt
a bit sleepy, and got my clothes on and marched downstairs, looked at the clock
and could not believe my own eyes, it was <u>a quarter to three!</u> So went back and
got into bed again and laid till <u>seven!</u> I don't know which would have been best,
early or late. I went to plough. At dinner-time, I went to the hill-top and saw a
truck of coals in at the station, so told William, as we expect a truck coming in
for Tomlinson's, but he thoought it would not be them. Tom and Thomas Pierson
came over as Ben is away at York at the fatstock show. It has been a fine day.*

December 11th Thursday

*I got up at six this morning - wasn't I a marvel - and guessed it, too, but it
was a mistake, I expected it would be seven. The truck of coals was Tomlinson's,
so we are going to lead them, but shall only get half a day, as Robinsons are going
to be on thrashing at the afternoon. We got two load up before dinner, then I went
to thrash. I was among the straw a bit, then I went among the corn. I was a bit
sruggled with the barley but managed to land through. We have been in
Thomas's yard, have got thrashed out down there now. My word, they have got a
gormless bullock. Such a nose and comical legs, but what can you expect out of
a turnip. They say old Wentworth of Newton is his father, no wonder he has been
only half got, or else too much so. At any rate, he has a most awful lump of a
nose.. Been a fine day.*

[Thomas Wentworth was gamekeeper to C.Richardson,Esq]

December 12th Friday

*Got up at six or so, did the horses and then I wrote a letter, instead of milking,
but I soon scribbled it over. After breakfast, I set off with the wagon for some
coals and William came after with the cart. I had got the wagon loaded when he
landed down. We only got three loads up but have loaded the wagon ready for
morning. I am going over to Lockton tonight all being well. I want a little box to
put my writing paper and such like things in, as they get very dirty throwing
about in the stable. It is a lovely moonlight night, but I don't think it is a frost.
Miss Keath has not been able to get churned today.*

December 13th Saturday

*Got up at six or so, did the horses and, after breakfast, William and I set off
for the station. We took the cart and left her at the station, then brought the
wagon up to the hill-top. We then brought a cart load up and put into her, then
went back for the rest and got them all on. It was rather late by we got home then,
after dinner, we both went to help to unload the coals. We brought the wagon
home, then set on to chop and also pulped some turnips with the engine. Welburn
had to churn and help with the butter making. We had to have a light to chop
with. I had the gramophone on at night. Robert Leng [Newton blacksmith] came
over and was here till late. Been a fine day.*

December 14th Sunday

*I did not get up this morning until I heard the eight o'clock bell going.
I started on the horses and finished them off after breakfast. William and I got*

some hay in - two good barrow loads - then I came home and it was dinner-time when I got there. Mr Pashby came up for his milk after dinner. Tom went out after dinner and did not land back till after nine. Hannah came to see us after tea but went back again. Our folks bought some apples from Brewers and I have eaten a nice lot today. I hear Aunt Ann is very bad with the blood poison in her arm, been at the doctor's today. Very fine day.

December 15th Monday

Up about half past six, had a bit of breakfast, then came over to Levisham. I got some more when I landed. I went to plough and have been ploughing all day. Our Tom came over at night to see William about money matters, as it is their rents on Wednesday. It seems a queer sort of going-on if a farm will not raise its own rent, but I think he does not do his duty by it, or it should do. I have written two letters today for lists, one for gramophones and another for diaries, will sent them off tomorrow. Been a fine day.

December 16th Tuesday

I did not get up this morning till seven,so had to hurry up a bit, but got into breakfast by eight. I went to plough afterwards and, by dinner-time, I brought my trace and things home, as I am not going to plough this afternoon.Instead, I went to pull some turnips and took a cart load of net stakes up and brought the turnips back, and by then it was night. After supper, Johnny Welburn and Arthur Magson came up. Johnny was blowing the cornet most of the time. They stayed till I had stabled up, then they went away. I have been nowhere tonight, have been writing my diary from Saturday last. Fine day, windy at night.

December 17th Wednesday

Got up this morning to see what time it was, it was ten minutes to five, so went back to bed and lay till half past six. Miss Keath had heard me and, at breakfast, she asked if it was me as she thought it was someone at the door. I have been ploughing all day. Tom came over at night and had a band practice. He had been at Pickering this morning and had got my watch, he brought it over with him. He bought a goose off Miss Keath and took it back with him. He has forgotten to bring my watch key, so I am having to borrow William's. Been a fine day.

December 18th Thursday

I had no bother this morning to get to know the time. Got up at six and did the horses. After breakfast, I went to plough. It does not plough very well, there are too many long stalks and brassocks. I sent away for a Grave's catalogue the other day and got it today, it is a very nice one and some very good machines are shown, I am thinking of getting one. I was over at Lockton at night, Johnny Welburn and Magson went with me. I got a lot of Christmas cards and a pencil. I told her I wanted a black one, but she has given me an old blue. [as his diary shows] It has been a lovely day, calm like spring.

December 19th Friday

I did not get up till nearly seven as it was a very dark morning, but it so happened that I had not to go out with the horses this morning as William said that I was to stay and help him to chop and pulp turnips. We were on all morning, fettling and one thing and another. After dinner, I had a bit of siding up to do and also had to go to meet the Tomlinsons off the three train with the luggage cart. I took two horses and there was a cart load of it. When I got back I did a few jobs and, after supper, Johnny Welburn and Magson came up and stayed with me till I got done. Very fine day.

December 20th Saturday

Got up about six, did the horses, then helped William to milk. After breakfast, I went to plough and have been ploughing all day. I have got it all done except a yard of a throwing-out piece and the headlands. I went round the headland just before it was dark and had a rum job to se what I was doing. At night, there was a band practice. Tom did not come, but William played the clarinet, they had a good practice. Miss Keath has been busy dressing geese, she has dressed four but was awfully late by she finished. The fox-hounds met here today. Fine day.

December 21st Sunday

Got up at half past seven, did the horses and also helped to milk. After breakfast, I got some hay in and then set off home, the people had already gone into church by then. I have not been anywhere today, been reading a good part of the time. Hannah came up at night to see us, she is at Newton yet, but has to go to the station as well, as Edie Woodmancy has had another son. We have not had Mr Pashby up today as they are away working at Sleights. It was rather a dull day, but fine. It will soon be Christmas.

December 22nd Monday

Got up about six or so, got ready and came over to Levisham, arrived about eight. Got my breakfast, then set off to plough. There had been a very heavy frost during the night and the plough would not go at all, so I loosed out and came to Swallowdale seeds. They are all right as there is a bit of cover on and the heavy plough, as well. Was ploughing all day but did not do much. William did not go into Pickering today. Tom came over at night, brought my boots over and a collar for Christmas day. Been a very fine day.

December 23rd Tuesday

Got up at half past six, did the horses and helped to milk. William said he would want me to help him among the sheep, so we went and it took us all morning to dig them a ford, as they had a full net ford, and we were among the turnips we hadn't got hoed, they were bad to do. We had intended going back after dinner, but the drain was blocked which takes the swig away from the pigstye, so we had to clean it out, a very dirty job. It took us both all the afternoon, as it is dark so soon. Betty was around at night looking for a hen she had lost, and she got hold of a stick which I had used among the swig and got all daubed, I did laugh!

December 24th Wednesday

Got up about six, did the horses and helped William to milk. After breakfast, I started to wash some turnips, at least, I went with the horse and cart for them first, then washed them ready for pulping, and we were on chopping as well. The engine went well. I did not go to bed, I had the gramophone on till twelve, then I went round with the band and held them the light, then got some supper when we got in again. Went to bed about two o'clock. It was a very fine night.

December 25th Thursday

Got up about seven and had a splitting headache and a very nasty sickly feeling in my stomach, could not eat any breakfast. William went round playing, our Tom was with them. They met at Farwath and went round by the new bridge and to Newton. I have been by myself so have not had a very good holiday. I never saw such dogy deed [?] in my life, it was worse than it is at our house. I was at church at night, had a rush to get there as I expected it started at seven, but it was at half past six. It was a drizzly sort of day and froze am making all very slape but it thawed before betime.

December 26th Friday

Got up at half past six, did the horses and helped to milk. Then I had to see to the sheep and the copper to set on, for the pig meat is all used. The band went round by Saltersgate and round home by Lockton, but have not played Lockton yet. I was kept going with one thing and another, boiled the copper five times and churned. I had the cows out a bit today for a run, but it came on wet in the afternoon so had to bring them in early. I have been down at the reading room tonight. It has been a fine morning, damp afternoon.

December 27th Saturday

Got up about six, did the horses, then helped to milk. After breakfast, finished off foddering then I went to the sheep. I had to start to drag them their food, got about a quarter of it done by dinner, it was a cold job. Was at it during the afternoon and have got half of it done. The band have been out today, they have played Levisham tonight but have Lockton to play yet. I have got a bit back with my writing as my pencil was such a bad one. I got it at Lockton and expected it was a lead pencil, but it was an old blue thing. [He is now writing with a lead one again] *Fine day but bitter cold.*

December 28th Sunday

Got up about half past seven, did the horses and also helped William to milk. After breakfast, I got some hay in, then I came home. Arrived about eleven, came up with Mr Pashby from Raindale. I did not go out either afternoon or night. Tom went out after dinner to Saintoft. Our folks have nobody staying this Christmas, they had expected Pollie and Jennie and families. Hannah came to see us after tea but had to go back again. It has been very cold all day and very much like some downfall, and it came on snowy about seven and I think it will snow all night.

December 29th Monday

Tom and I were talking till late last night after we got to bed, so I was a trifle lazy around getting-up time and, besides, it was snowing and had got a lot down, so I did not go to Levisham this morning but went at dinner-time, instead. The Stape band was going to Pickering today but only half of them gathered at the station, so postponed it till next week. They could not have stood out playing this morning, but it got out fine during the afternoon. I went up to the sheep when I got to Levisham, as William had gone to Pickering, and was digging their ford all afternoon. I only got a few rows done, as it was bad to do and it was cold as well. Snowy morning, better afternoon.

December 30th Tuesday

I did not get up very soon as there was no need to, seeing I could not get out with the horses. There had been some more snow and it is almost a foot and a half thick all over, there are no drifts as yet. I had to go to the sheep with some hay, and was busy setting stakes for the next ford, William was mending the net at home. After dinner, I took the sheep some more hay and pulled a few turnips. Had to shovel the snow off them first as you cannot see the rows. Only got about half a cart load, brought them home at night. I went to Lockton for some New Year cards and also bought a lead pencil, one of the right kind this time. fine day, but cold.

December 31st Wednesday

It had been a bit windy during the night and had blown all the tracks up, but there are no drifts, though it is very bad to walk among, you slip about so, it is small frozen stuff. William and I went to the sheep and set a couple of nets. It was a cold job as the nets were all frozen, as it had been freezing all night. At dinner time, the Stape band came through, they sounded very good. During the afternoon, William and I went to pull turnips. We had the snow to shovel off them first, but got a good big cart load and got them home. I was down at the reading room at night, they are busy decorating for the children's party on Friday. Very fine day. Well, this is the end of another year and, taking it all together, it has been a very good year as far as I am concerned.

Memoranda

Saw a primrose out in flower in Smith Wood on Sunday, Mar 16, also a dandelion in flower in the bull field hedgeside, Levisham, Wed Mar 19. Heard the cuckoo for the first time as I was lighting a fire in the lingey field, Apr 29. Drilled swedes May 22 at Levisham, finished drilling altogether on Jul 8. Started hay time Jul 12, finished Aug 6. Started harvest Aud 29, started reaper Aug 30, finished reaping Sep 1, started to lead Sep 9, finished leading Sep 13. Started to sleep horses in Oct 7. Started to plough Oct 8. Sowed our wheat Oct 28. Started to plough seeds Nov 17.

CASH ACCOUNT

January At the commencement of the year I had 10/-   February

	Rec'd		Paid		Rec'd		Paid
7th	1/3/0	Band money	3/6	7th		Basket to Whitby	6
13th		Lent Hannah		7th		Sunday Companion	1
15th		Melodeon repairs	6	6th		Parcel for Hannah	4
18th		Lent Hannah	2/6	12th		Sweets	2
20th		Spent at Pickering	4/0	15th		Sweets & matches	3
25th		Towards kippers	3½	15th	4/0	Work at Keath's	
25th		Things from man at door	4	24th		Nine insurance stamps	5/3
26th		Sunday collection	1	24th		Sweets & oranges	7
29th		Postal order for Pollie	1/7	24th		Train (?)	8
30		Postage stamps	2	24th		Carbine	6
29th		For meat & stamps	2/1			Death insurance	1/6
31st		Basket to Jannie & postage stamp	6			Sweets at Levisham	2
						1 week's insurance	4
	1/13/0		*15/7½*		*4/0*		*10/4*

March				April			
	Rec'd		Paid		Rec'd		Paid
1st	16/0	2 weeks wages at Keaths			1/0	From Hannah for sum lent in January	
1st		Oranges	2	3rd		For suit, J.Simpson	1/10/0
1st		Sweets	3	5th	8/8	Week's wage less insurance	
1st		Drink	6				
		Pair of new shoes	16/6	5th		Sweets	2
1st		2 weeks insurance	8			Paid for Tom at Sedman's	6/6
5th		Mints	2				
8th		Sweets	4			Paid for my own account	1/3
8th	8/3	1 week's wages		16th		Train fare to Pickering	10
8th		Insurance	4				
9th		"	4				

9th		Sweets	4			Tea 6d,book 3d,book 1d,sweets 1d,cotton wool 3d,post card 1d	1/3
9th		Collection	1½				
9th		Jennie got	4/0				
17th		Oranges	1			Death insurance	7
		Sweets	1			Collection	1
		Supper at Stape	6			"	+
		Collection	3	26th		Spent at Dales (?)	6
		Sweets, cocoa	6½			For repair of Sunday boots	1/0
	7/0	Week's wage as I have knocked 2/- off for good					
	£1/11/3		£1/5/2		9/8		£2/2/2½

May				June			
	Rec'd		Paid		Rec'd		Paid
3rd	13/6	For 3 week's work				Collection Cropton Anniversary	1½
		For 3 week's insurance	1/0				
7th		For cough sweets	2	7th	9/0	Week's wage	
		Train fare to Grosmont	1/0			Week's insurance	4
		Sweets from shop at Egton Bridge	2			Pair of yellow shoes	13/6
		"	3			2 hats,1tweed 1.6d,1 soft green felt 3/11d	4/5
		Sweets from stall	2			6 collars 3.0d, 3fronts 1.6d	4/6
		Ice cream	1			2 ties 2/-,1bow 6+d,handkerchief 6+d	3/1
		Shot at coconuts,got none	2			1 smock 2.11d, pair braces 1/-	3/11
11th		Our meeting, gave for missionaries	5			Pump valve 4d, repair outfit 6d	10
12th	3/0	For playing at Egton Bridge				Sweets	2
17th	12/9	Fortnight's wages		14th	9/0	Week's wage	
		" insurance	8	14th		Week's insurance	4
23rd		Postal order to pay Mr Simpson	18/0	15th		Tea at Stape	6
		Sweets	2	15th		Hymn sheet collection	2
		Stamp	1	18th		Orange	1
		Postal order	1½	21st	9/0	Week's wage	
		Sweets	2			Week's insurance	4
		Week's insurance	4			Sweets	2
25th		Paid at Burnetts	6	28th	9/0	Week's wage	
28th		Sweets	3			Week's insurance	4
		Brass polish	1			Pair of new shoes	8/11
31st	9/0	Week's wage				2 pairs stockings	2/3
		Week's insurance	4			Boot laces 1d,buttons1d	2
						Fried fish 2d,sweets 2d	4
	2/7/3		1/3/11½		1/16/0		2/4/5½

July				August			
	Rec'd		Paid		Rec'd		Paid
5th	9/0	Week's wage		2nd		Levisham show,into field	6
5th		Week's insurance	4	2nd		" " sweets	4
5th		Sweets	2	2nd		" " tea	1
4th		Gave Harold for the hare	6	2nd		" " entrance	3
						walking match	
7th		Sweets from Lockton 3d, from Dales 1d	4	2nd		Levisham show,hat trimming 2d,thrashing 2d	4

Date	Rec'd	Item	Paid
13th		Gave Polly's children	4½
		Spent at Burnetts	6
19th	9/0	Week's wage	
19th		Week's insurance 4d, sweets 2d	6
24th		Gave the boy 1d, sweets 1d	
26th	9/0	Week's wage, insurance	4
	1/7/0		**3/2½**

Date	Rec'd	Item	Paid
2nd		Levisham show, 3-legged race	2
	2/6	Levisham show, got for hat trimming	
2nd		Levisham show, guessing competition	2
10th		Sunday collection	1
14th		Sweets	1
18th		Train to Whitby	2/3
18th		Silver watch chain 4/6d, 1 medal 1/6d	6/0
18th		Fountain pen	1/0
18th		Combination glass	1/0
18th		Dinner 7d, tea 5d, sweets 8d	1/8
18th		Post cards 6d, whistle 6d, ices 2d	1/2
18th		Mouth organ 1/,- catalogue 2d	1/2
18th		Plums 4d, museum 3d	7
31st		Gave Hannah for Mr Milestone for quarter day	1/0
9th	16/0	Fortnight's wages	
		Fortnight's insurance	8
16th	9/0	Week's wage, week's insurance	4
23rd	6/0	" " "	4
30th	9/0	" " "	4
	2/2/6		**18/3**

September

Date	Rec'd	Item	Paid
1st		Train to Pickering	10
1st		Gloves 1.6d, leather gaiters 6d, boot laces 2d, sweets 2d	2/0
1st		Cake for tea 5d, buttons 1d,	6
1st		Teeth out	3/0
1st		Haircut & shave	3
6th	12/0	Harvest wage. Insurance	4
13th	18/0	" " "	4
18th	1/0	Mr Armstrong gave me for leading	
20th	18/0	Week's wage. Insurance	4
21st		Gave William back, as we had done harvest	3
21st		Gave Stephen Eddon, also gave ½ away	1½
23rd	3	I found up Morly Lane	
27th	9/0	Week's wage. Insurance	4
	2/17/3		**8/7½**

October

Date	Rec'd	Item	Paid
2nd		Sweets at Lockton	6
4th	9/0	Week's wage. Insurance	4
4th		Sweets 2d, matches 1d	3
6th		Gave Hannah for some new shirts	10/0
7th	6	Mr Tomlinson gave me	
11th	9/0	Week's wage. Insurance	4
14th		Spent at the thanksgiving	3/3
17th		Gave the boys for 5th November	4
18th	6/0	Week's wage. Insurance	4
18th		Pair of new shoes	11/6
18th		Ordered 1doz. postcard photos	3/3
18th		¼ lb toffee 4d, sweets 2d	6
20th		Gave Pollie for making shirts	2/6
25th	7/0	Week's wage. Insurance	4
28th		Sweets at Lockton 6d, Spanish 1d	7
	1/12/0		**1/14/0**

Tom has been in my drawer at home and has got 5/-

November Rec'd			Paid
1st	9/0	Week's wage.Insurance	4
2nd		Gave mother	1/0
2nd		Bought 2 rabbits from Harold	8
2nd	1/0	Sold Harold pair of old boots	
8th	9/0	Week's wage.Insurance	4
16th		Bought a cap from Harold	1/0
22nd	18/0	Fortnight's wages. Insurance	4
24th		Train fare to Pickering	10
24th		Bought top coat	15/6
24th		Sweets 3d,coconuts 4d	7
24th		Watch chain 6½d, purse 6½d	1/1
24th		Two pocket knives	1/0
24th		Two rides on the horses	2
24th		Into show 2d, cinematograph show 3d	5
	1/6	Got off Tom	
30th		Sleightholme collection	2
30th		Gave mother	6
	1/18/6		1/4/3

December Rec'd			Paid
6th		Sweets	6
9th		Gave Magson towards gramophone	1/0
13th	15/10	Fortnight's wages less insurance	
13th		Got some picture postcards	1/0
18th		Got some Christmas cards & a pencil	1/0
18th		Also got some sweets	2
19th		Sent Jennie some money she wrote for	9/0
19th	1/0	Tip from Mr Tomlinson	
20th	9/0	Week's wage.Insurance	4
30th		3 New Year cards 3d, lead pencil ½d	3½
30th		Pair of boot laces	2
31st		Two ½d stamps	1
19th		Jennie's order stamp	1
9th			
	1/5/10		19/1½

John Brough
c/o Mr Keath,
Levisham,
Pickering, Yorks.   I had £5/10/0 in the bank by Nov 24th.

GLOSSARY

bass	straw basket
boak	balk; ridge dividing ploughed land
brassocks	charlock
dess (of hay)	truss or block
fog	second crop of grass, following mowing
fur	furrow
gays	irregular pieces at edges of plouged fields
manishment	fertilizer
prod	stick used in thatching
pyke	small round stack of corn or straw
quart (vb)	to plough a second time, going across the furrows
rigg	ridge
roak (roke)	mist
rully	low-sided cart or dray
scruffle (vb)	to weed between rows with horse-drawn scruffler
segrams	ragwort
slape	slippery
slipe	cut
snig (vb)	to haul or drag out, esp. timber
wicks	couch grass
winder (vb)	to winnow

NOTES

Sources

Brough, John	Diary for the year 1913 MS in possession of John Brough,12,Yearlsley Cres.,York
Watson, John	The Rector's Son; or Memoirs of Mr.John Skelton. pub 1833 London
Walker, H.,J., & B.M.	Recollections pub.Richard Jackson Ltd..Leeds.1930
Walker, B.M.	The Well of Life pub.Wildblood & Ward, Leeds 1939

Background information on the people and events relating to the three documents has been found in :-

*Census Returns for Levisham & NewtonFarm Survey 1941	PRO
*Levisham Parish Registers	North Yorkshire County Record Office (NYCRO)
*Levisham Tithe Map 1848	
*Levisham : 1910 Valuation	NYCRO
*Levisham : Pauper Book	
Register of Deeds	NYCRO
Methodist Magazines	John Ryland Library, Manchester
Methodist Circuit Plans	NYCRO & John Ryland Library
Malton Messenger	Malton Library
Wills	Borthwick Institute, York
Yorkshire Gazette	Malton Library

Copies of transcripts of documents marked * can be seen, by arrangement, in the collection of Local History Archives in Levisham Village Hall

BIBLIOGRAPHY

Archbishop Herring's Visitation	Yorks Archaeological Soc.
Atkinson, Rev .J.C	Forty Years in a Moorland Parish M.T.D. Rigg.1992
Baker, Frank	Methodism & the Love Feast. Epworth 1957
Fream, W.	Elements of Agriculture 1892
Hartley, Marie & Ingilby, Joan	Life & Traditions in The Moorlands of North-East Yorkshire, Smith Settle 1990
Hayes, R.H.	Levisham Moor: Archaeological Investigations 1957-1978.N.Y.Moors National Parks Committe & Scarborough Archaeological & Historical Soc 1929 1983
Kellett,Arnold	The Yorkshire Dictionary. Smith Settle 1994
Marshall.W	Rural Economy of Yorkshire 1788
North Riding Records	New Series R.B.Turton 1897
Owen, John S.	Walker's Pit in Newton Dale. Cleveland Industrial Archaeologist 1994 no 22 pp.39-46
Rushton, J.H.	They kept Faith. Beck Isle Museum pub.
Strong, Ruth	Methodism in a Moorland Village Unpublished MS
Wesley, John	Journal. Everyman ed., Dent 1906

REFERENCES

1   Hayes. pp.24-5
2   N.Riding Records I.p.102; II.pp. 15,42; III.p.158
3.   Owen pp. 39-46
4   Archbishop Herring vol.2. p.152
5.   NYCRO 1828 Non Conformist Places of Worship Micro 483
6.   Strong
7.   Baker
8   Wesley vol 3 p.69
9   Atkinson p.15
10   Rushton p.97
11   Levisham Pauper Book: in letter to Charity Commission 1883 re. money administered by Robert Skelton, "....1855 about which time his estate and affairs passed into liquidation in Bankruptcy."
12   Rev. John Mercer, Minister in Pickering Circuit 1831-2. (Circuit Plan : John Ryland Library)
13   Hartley & Ingilby pp.83-85
14   1910 Valuation
15   Farm Survey 1941
16   Hatley & Ingilby pp.48-50, and Fream pp.40-44
17   Marshall pp.132-134.
Cisterns collecting rain water were the normal water supply in Levisham until 1895 when piped water was brought to standpipes in the village.At a meeting of the Pickering Poor Law Guardians on Aug.31 1894,it was reported that Levisham had 116 inhabitants and "there is not a well in the place. Residents depend on rainwater or fetching water from the stream which is 300ft below the lowest house and 800-900 yards distant. Last year's drought was severe and residents had petitioned for better water......The only known spring is 270 ft below the centre of the village and belongs to Mrs Heslop, widow of the late incumbent, who agrees to its use. it has been decided to use a waterwheel which will be placed in the stream , a concrete dam made to form a race. Alongside will be a rubble gathering well to which water will be piped in cast iron lead-jointed pipes for the spring, and for the well it will be pumped to a reservoir at the highest point of the village by a road and thence to 3 standpipes. The reservoir to be cylindrical 12 ft diameter and 10 ft deep with a manhole. It would have a 7,062 gallons capacity which would allow one week's reserve supply." PRO
18   Hartley & Ingilby pp.76-81

INDEX